HAPPY TAPPING

with Charlie

Paula Kennedy

Energy EFT for kids

All rights are reserved in all media, including future media. No part of this book may be reproduced or transmitted in any format, whether mechanical or electronic. This includes recordings, photography or by any kind of storage or revival system without prior written permission from myself (Paula Kennedy) 2017 the author and copyright owner.

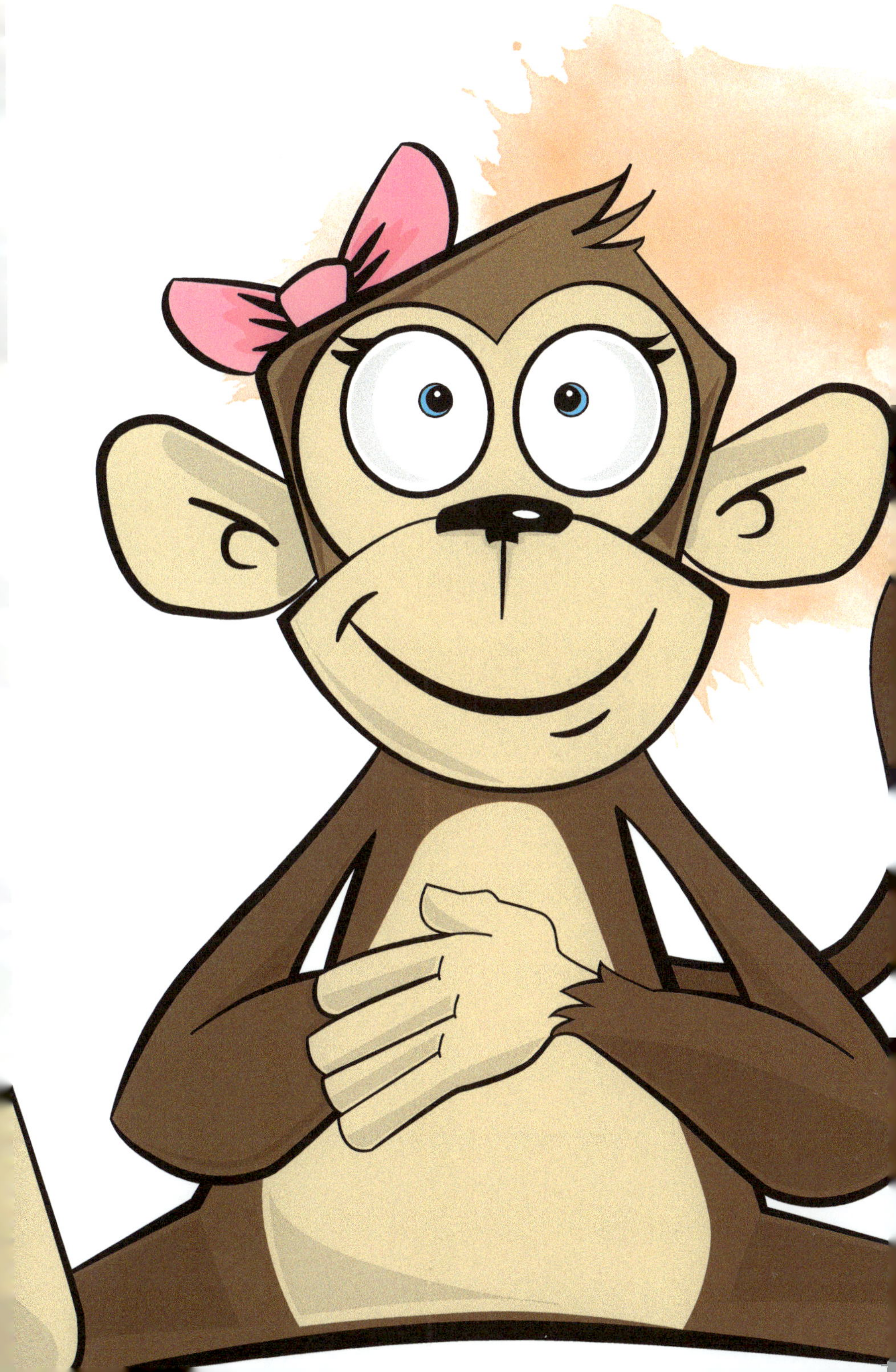

CONTENTS

Information for Mum, Dad,
Teachers, Carer Workers.   2

How EFT (tapping) works and how to use
the Tapping Points   5

Mia Monkey and the magic of Energy EFT   13

Going to Bed   17

Feeling Grumpy   27

Little accidents   37

Starting pre school/school   51

Friendships   61

Little Fallouts with friends	71
Separation Anxiety	79
Fear of the dark	89
Losing a pet	99
Fear of creepy crawlies/spiders	109
Silent Tapping	119
Mia Monkeys Tapping song	129
Additional Reading	133

REVIEW

I practice and teach EFT so I know from experience the amazing benefits children and adults alike can get from EFT.

Paula Kennedy has written an attractive and well thought out book for young children. She is passionate about spreading the word about EFT to children and teenagers and it is reflected in the book.

The use of Mia Monkey and Charlie Chameleon to show the tapping points and the range of feeling is a marvellous idea and it will encourage children to do what "they say". This book is simple, attractive and very helpful to introduce tapping to young children.

Francoise Gins

EFT practitioner & trainer

DISCLAIMER

The contents of this self-help book are purely for educational purposes only. This information should not be used to replace medical help, advice, or be a substitute for any medical or psychological condition. Always consult your doctor or other medical health professional if in any doubt.

This self-help children's book is a gentle introduction to the therapy EFT (Emotional Freedom Technique). It is written in a format that is simple for adults, teachers and children to understand and access. It is also a good reference for parents, teachers and care workers. It is advisable for a parent, care worker or teacher to read through with a child under the age of 18. Parents, teachers and care workers, may also greatly benefit from using the contents of this book to relieve their daily stresses. Group tapping sessions can be very beneficial for all the family or in the classroom.

Although the results and clinical trials of using EFT have been very encouraging and very positive, it is still in its early years of development, therefore anyone using this book is totally responsible for their own well-being.

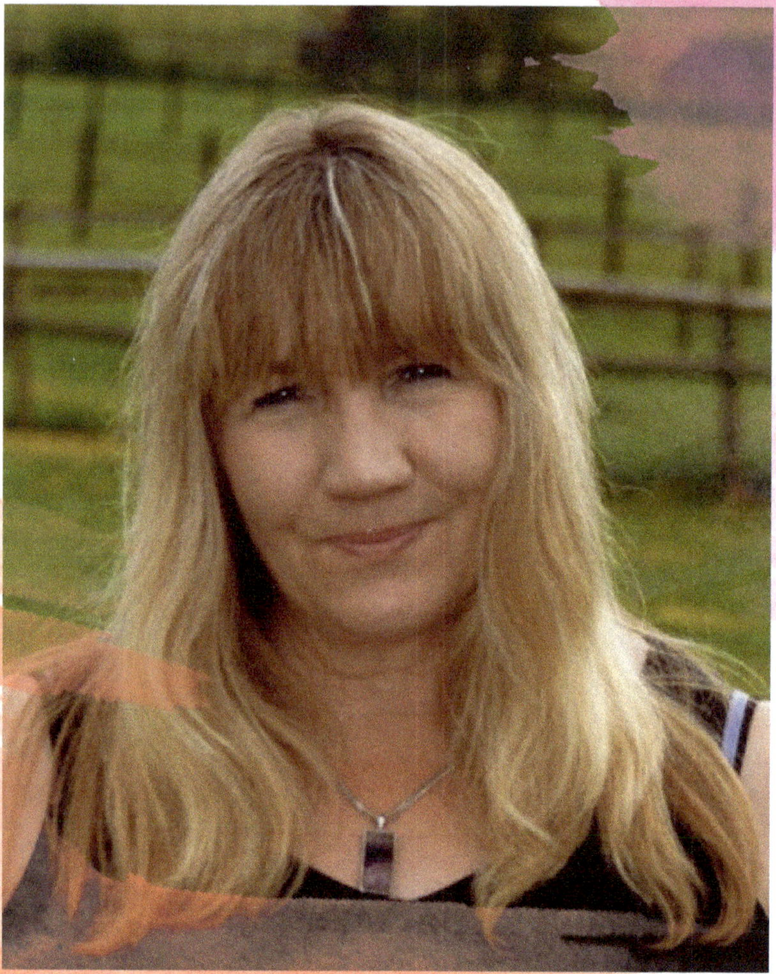

ABOUT THE AUTHOR

I am firstly a mum of three wonderful daughters, two of whom are on the Autistic Spectrum and the other a saint/angel for coping so well with it all. They are my inspiration for writing this book and also my first book Energy EFT For Teenagers which is currently available on Amazon, therefore sharing the magic that EFT can bring to other children's/families' lives.

I am also an artist, an author, a carer, a horse/animal rescuer and rehabilitator, a Reiki Master Practitioner and an Energy EFT Master Practitioner and over the years have learned to become a problem solver when the answers just didn't seem to be out there for the dilemmas our family was facing.

The reason for me writing Happy Tapping with Mia & Charlie and also my first book Energy EFT For Teenagers, is to provide functional help to other mums, dads, children, families, care workers/givers and schools where there seems to be little or no help when things go wrong in one way or another. Things can hopefully be improved, by using this profound but simple tapping therapy called Energy EFT in our daily lives.

I have lived and breathed the contents of this book, it is all written from experience and from my searching for answers for myself and my own children when life didn't go quite to plan.

As a family we have faced many problems head on, they include, Selective Mutism, Sensory Processing Disorder, Aspergers, School Phobia, Severe Anxiety, Bullying, Eating Disorders,

Grief/trauma, Extreme Stress, Low Self Esteem, Social Anxiety etc, but we have triumphed and my girls are all growing up and thriving. Our family life is as stress free and happy as we can make it.

MY MISSION

Mia Monkey, Charlie Chameleon and I are on a mission to spread the word and use of Energy EFT. I hope my little book will help to introduce Energy EFT to children and families, and I would love to see it used in pre schools/schools to help children with Going to Bed, Feeling Grumpy, Little Accidents, Starting Pre School/School, Friendships and Fallouts, Separation Anxiety, Fear of the Dark and Fear of Creepy Crawlies/Spiders, losing a beloved Pet and also Silent Tapping if your child is anxious about talking about their problems. Please read it, use it, share it, talk about it and hopefully your children will greatly benefit from it.

THANKS

To Nick Klynsmith for all the wonderful graphics and for creating Mia Monkey and Charlie Chameleon.

To my three wonderful daughters, Sophie, Daisy and Millie Kennedy for teaching me that being a Mum has many challenges but also many amazing moments and treasured memories. Also for being the inspiration to write Happy Tapping with Mia & Charlie so that it may help other children with any problems they may encounter while growing up.

To my beautiful mum, Erin Fryer, who has stood by, supported and trialled all my therapies and helped me when I dealt with the challenges of having children on the Autistic Spectrum. Also for being there for me through thick and thin.

To my kind, loving partner, Julian Gammon, for helping me through all of what life has thrown at us and still being there on the other side.

Also many thanks to Gary Craig, Silvia Hartmann for the SUE Scale, and my wonderful EFT trainer Francoise Gins because without them I would never have started this amazing journey.

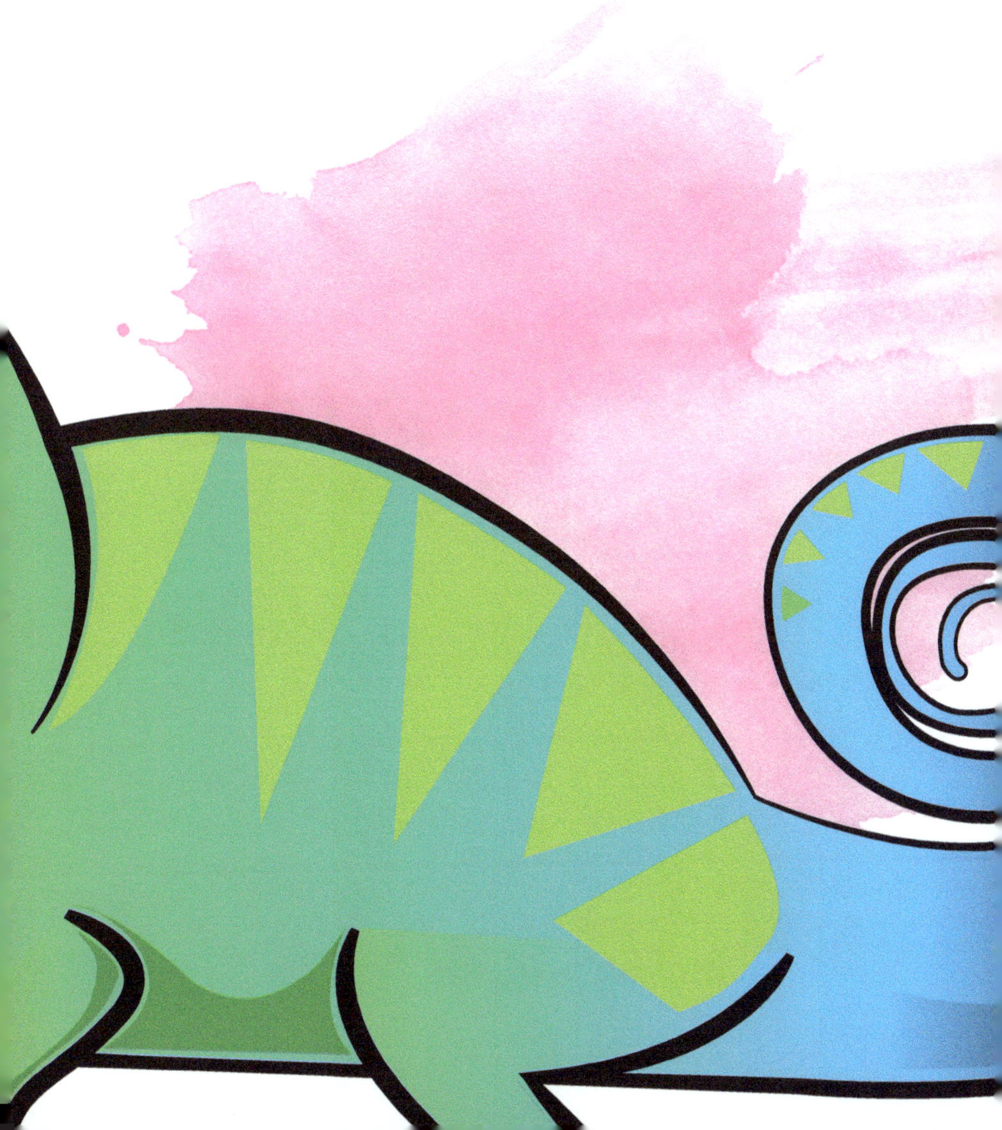

INFORMATION FOR MUM, DAD, TEACHERS, CARER WORKERS.

Mia Monkey has tapping points on her head body and hands and so do we. These are called meridian points and we have used them for thousands of years in the form of Acupuncture or Acupressure and now, using EFT (Emotional Freedom Technique). We use our fingers to very gently tap these points to help us to feel calm and less stressed or anxious. By tapping the points there is recent scientific evidence that we gently calm the Amygdala in the brain which helps to melt away any tension, stress, fear, anxiety, grief and unwanted emotions. EFT is a very useful 'first aid' therapy/tool for children/teenagers and adults to have in their tool box, we can use it any time, any place, anywhere and it is literally at our fingertips to help when the need arises.

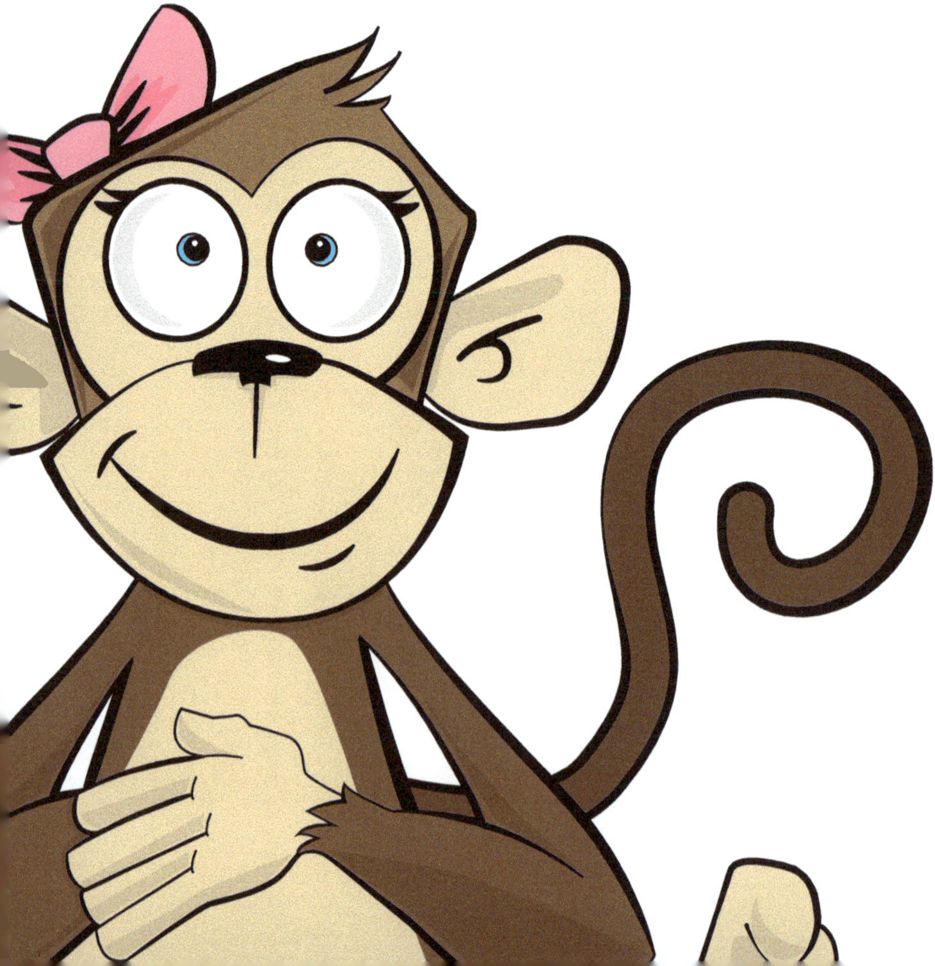

HOW EFT (TAPPING) WORKS AND HOW TO USE THE TAPPING POINTS

Mia Monkey shows you how to use the tapping points. All of the points are marked on Mia Monkey's face, collarbone point and hand points with little red hearts.

Mia Monkey simply starts the tapping process by very gently tapping the top of the head point, then she taps the middle of the forehead point, onto the inner eyebrow point, then to the side of the eye point, moving down to the under the eye point, then down the face further to the under the nose point, on to the under the mouth point, then to the collarbone point, From there we move on to the hand points starting with the thumbnail point and we gently tap through to each of our fingernail points, to the karate chop point using the other hand to tap.

To make it easier for children to learn the tapping points and how to tap through a script, I have written the book a bit like the copying game **'Simon Says'**. Also there is a little song/rhyme to help them learn remember the points.

Tapping is a life long skill/tool that once learned, children can then use in any situation where they feel worried, anxious, angry, scared, bored, fed up etc.

When we use EFT we tap on specific points on the head, collar bone and hand, use a set up statement and a script, to help release any unwanted emotions or negative energy we are carrying in our body. It is simply like clearing out our back pack or toy box and getting rid of things we no longer want or need, making us feel happy again. By gently tapping on negative emotions we slowly release them to create a positive result, helping us to feel better.

Mia Monkey has a special friend called Charlie Chameleon. Charlie has a number scale to help us gauge how we are feeling at that moment. If we feel angry or sad or anxious our emotions could show up somewhere on the minus side of Charlie Chameleon's scale. If we were feeling really good then we would more likely be higher up on the plus side of Charlie Chameleon's scale, or anywhere in between. At a minus 10, we could be feeling so bad that we might not want to get out of bed and at a plus 10 we could be having the most amazing day ever possible. At neutral or zero we would feel neutral and not feel very much at all.

feeling low → feeling nothing → feeling great

-10 -9 -8 -7 -6 -5 -4 -3 -2 -1 0 +1 +2 +3 +4 +5 +6 +7 +8 +9 +10

By gauging how we feel on Charlie Chameleon's scale, we will notice how much better we are feeling each time we tap through a sequence. We hope to get our numbers up into the plus side of the scale so we feel much better about whatever has been troubling us. Sometimes we may need to repeat the tapping script several times to get our numbers into the plus side of the scale, so we let go of all the unwanted emotion and feel much better.
Mia Monkey and Charlie Chameleon will show us how.

Before we do each round of tapping Mia Monkey crosses her hands across her heart into the heart healing position. She shuts her eyes and takes three deep breaths,

in and out,

in and out,

in and out.

This is a very important part of the tapping process as it allows us to let go of all that unwanted emotion and if we are in a position where we are unable to tap then the heart healing position just gives us a moment to be in the here and now, we can cross our hands over our heart and breathe deeply in and out three times to help us relax and calm our nerves and anxieties.

Mia Monkey gives the tapping session a title e.g.

'I'm not tired'.

Then Mia Monkey starts to do some EFT 'tapping'. Just follow along like the game 'Simon Says'.

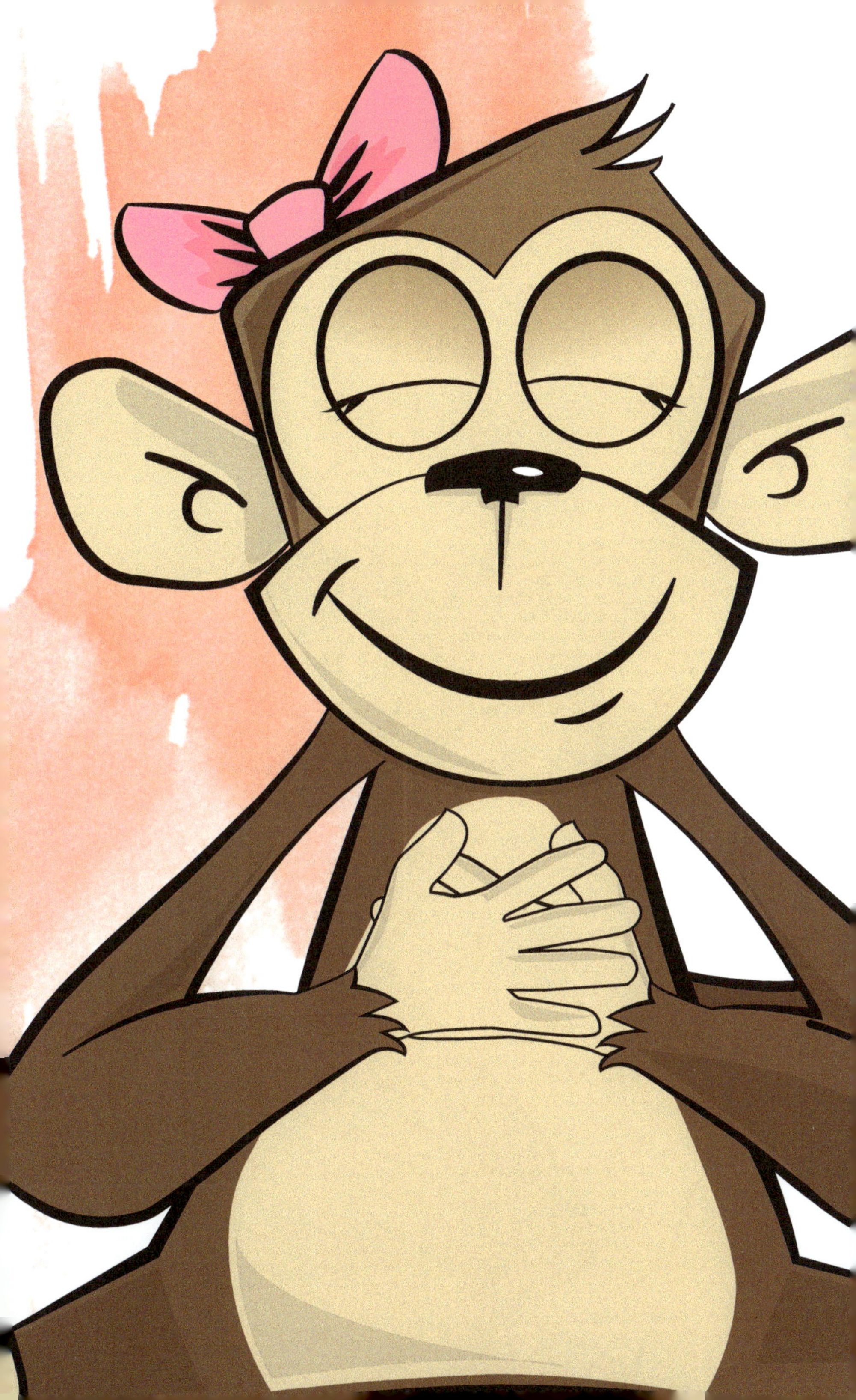

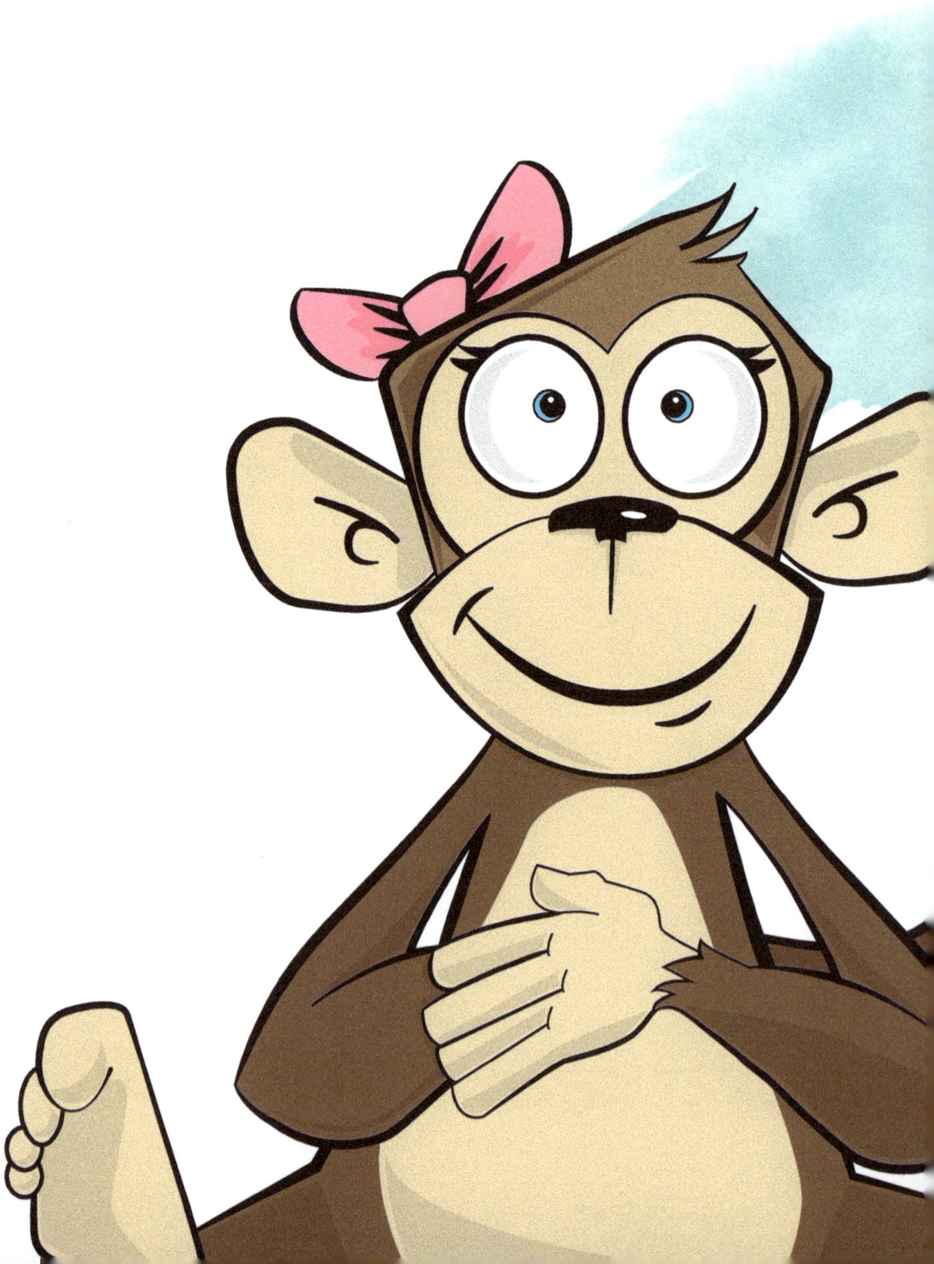

MIA MONKEY AND THE MAGIC OF ENERGY EFT

This is the story of Mia Monkey and how she uses the magic of EFT to help children. By using EFT, Mia Monkey helps children that can't get to sleep or are worried about certain things.

Mia Monkey says 'Hi' – she wants to know what you are worried about today?

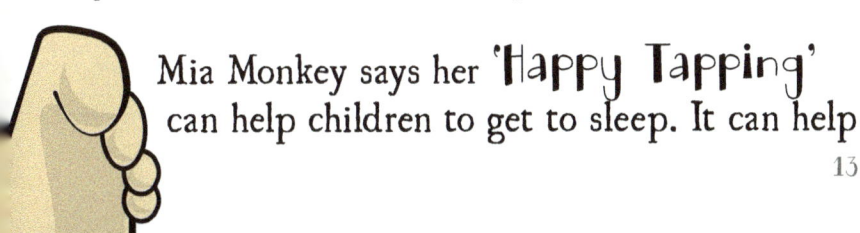

Mia Monkey says her 'Happy Tapping' can help children to get to sleep. It can help if they get grumpy or anxious about new things, with life's little accidents, making new friends, fallouts with existing friends or starting a new school. Mia Monkey has added a script on losing a beloved pet, the words could be changed for this if the child sadly loses a friend or family member to help them cope with the loss. It can even help if they get scared of the dark, or scared of bugs or spiders. Children can also do some 'silent tapping' and tune into the feelings in their body if they don't feel like talking about their problems, opening a window for being brave enough to talk about what is bothering them later on.

Mia Monkey says she has an **imaginary safety vest and an imaginary safety blanket** they have a little pocket over her heart. Mia Monkey says when anyone says or does anything mean to her she shuts the door tight and shuts the negative words or feelings out, and when someone says or does something nice she opens the little door and lets them into her heart. This is a lovely way for your child to feel safe, protected and in control of situations, they have the power to shut out negative thoughts and feelings that could otherwise make them sad. Mia Monkey says your safety vest and blanket are imaginary and no one else can see them but you, so you can use them anytime the need arises. Mia Monkey says, come on lets put on our **imaginary safety vest** and do some **Super Tapping**.

Mia Monkey says she has written down some of the things that might worry you from time to time.

Shall we have a look at what they are?

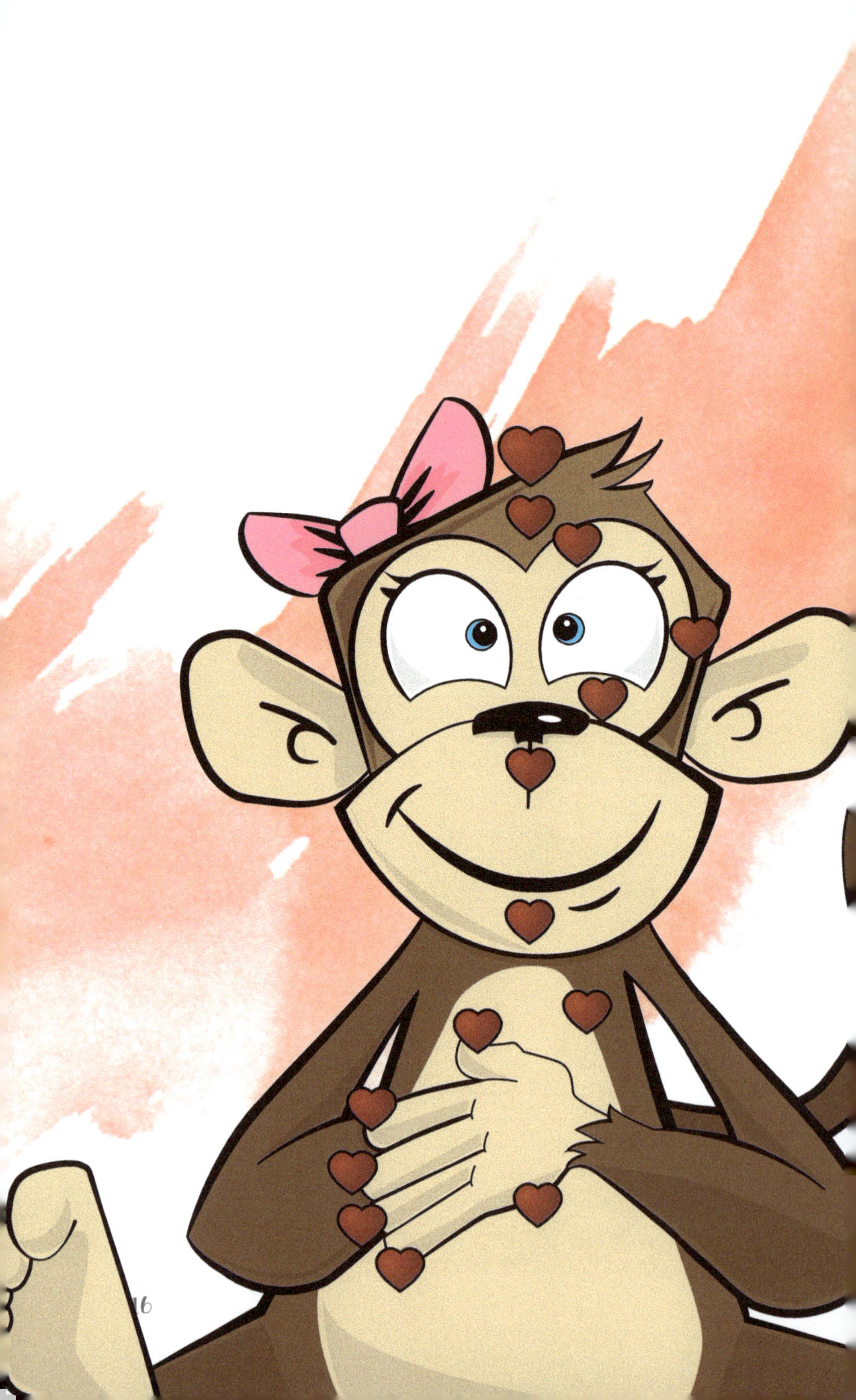

GOING TO BED

Mia Monkey says going to bed can be a little bit hard sometimes especially if we can't get to sleep. Mia Monkey says she has an **imaginary safety blanket** that she takes to bed and wraps around herself under her duvet, her **imaginary safety blanket** helps her to feel safe and snugly, as it is in her imagination no one else can see it.

Mia Monkey says you too can have an **imaginary safety blanket,** so wrap yourself up and lets get ready to go to sleep.

Mia Monkey says she knows a fun way to try to get to sleep, it's a simple little game called '**Mia Monkey Says**', so just copy what Mia Monkey says and do some 'Happy Tapping', it's a little bit like the game '**Simon Says**'.

Mia Monkey says 'cross your hands over your heart in the heart healing position and take three deep breaths,

in and out,

in and out,

in and out.

Name your title out loud, 'I'm not tired'. Now copy Mia Monkey and do some magic tapping!

Mia Monkey says tap where I tap and repeat after me.

I'm not tired.

Mia Monkey says tap the top of your head very gently 5 times.

I'm still full of beans.

Mia Monkey says tap the middle of your forehead very gently 5 times.

I don't want to go to sleep.

Mia Monkey says tap your inner eyebrow very gently 5 times.

I want to stay up longer.

Mia Monkey says tap the outside of your eye very gently 5 times.

Please let me stay up?

Mia Monkey says tap under your eye very gently 5 times.

I promise to be good?

Mia Monkey says tap under your nose very gently 5 times.

Just for a little while longer?

Mia Monkey says tap under your mouth very gently 5 times.

Do I have to go to bed?

Mia Monkey says tap your collarbone very gently 5 times.

Maybe I do feel a little bit tired, yawn.

Mia Monkey says tap your thumbnail with another finger gently 5 times.

I am starting to feel sleepy.

Mia Monkey yawns and says tap your index fingernail with another finger gently 5 times.

So sleepy and snugly in my lovely bed.

Mia Monkey says tap your middle fingernail with another finger gently 5 times.

I love my bed, it's so cosy and warm.

Mia Monkey says tap your ring fingernail with another finger gently 5 times.

Feeling so sleepy and tired.

Mia Monkey says tap your little fingernail with another finger gently 5 times.

Sleepy, tired and relaxed, big yawn!

Mia Monkey says tap your karate chop with another finger 5 times.

Now place your hands across your heart in the heart healing position and take three deep breaths with Mia Monkey,

in and out,
in and out,
in and out,

then just relax.

Aaaah, that feels better, Mia Monkey feels another big yawn coming,

YAWN,

and another one
YAWN

and another
YAWN.

feeling low → feeling nothing → feeling great

-10 -9 -8 -7 -6 -5 -4 -3 -2 -1 0 +1 +2 +3 +4 +5 +6 +7 +8 +9 +10

Mia Monkey says do you feel sleepy yet, she says how sleepy do you feel on Charlie Chameleon's number scale? Have a look at the numbers on Charlie Chameleon's scale you could possibly be a -2 or a -1 if you are not feeling sleepy yet, choose a number that relates to how sleepy you are feeling.

Mia Monkey hopes you will feel sleepy enough to go to sleep but if you are still a little bit awake then repeat the tapping lines again a few times until you are on the plus side of Charlie Chameleon's scale and are feeling sleepy enough to drift off into a lovely sleep. Mia Monkey says 'snuggle under your imaginary safety blanket and duvet and feel really comfy, safe and warm'.

Maybe you are already asleep? says Mia Monkey, 'this little sleepy person has drifted off to sleep, night night sleepy head.'

Mia Monkey is really tired too, she is drifting off to sleep with you.

Night night Mia Monkey,

night night Charlie Chameleon.

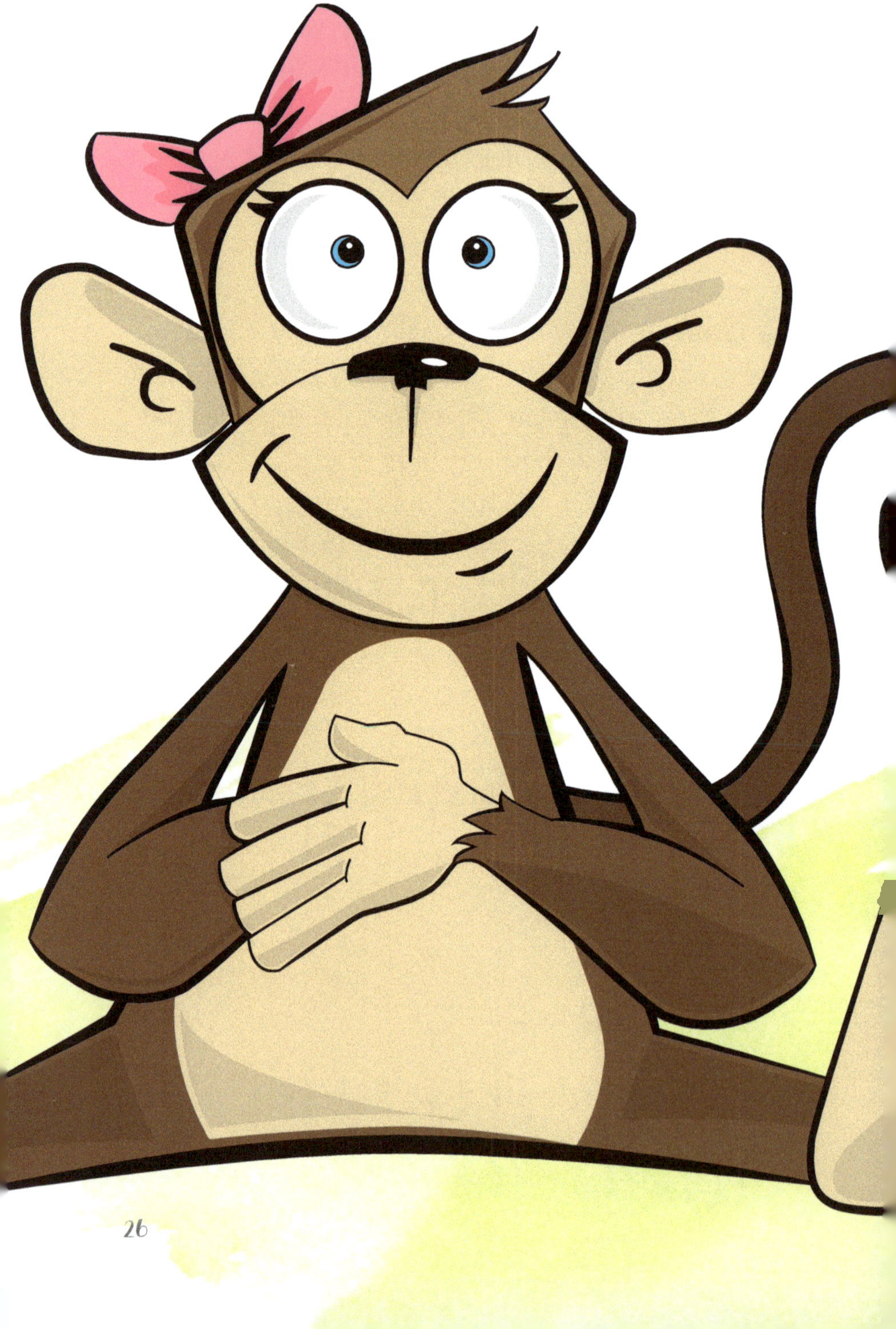

FEELING GRUMPY

Mia Monkey says sometimes we can feel a little bit grumpy. Shall we tap along with Mia Monkey until we feel a bit better? Mia Monkey says a little bit of 'Happy Tapping' should make us feel much better,

aaaaah!

Mia Monkey says this is a great time to zip up your **imaginary safety vest** and shut out anything that has makes you cross or sad. Are you all zipped up and ready to make things feel better?

Measure how grumpy you are feeling on Charlie Chameleon's scale and remember your number so we can hopefully see a change after a few rounds of tapping. If you feel really grumpy you will probably be on the minus side of the scale. Let's see if Charlie Chameleon can get you get into the happy positive side of his scale.

Let's tap along with Mia Monkey, to help us feel better. Are you ready to use your tapping fingers?

feeling low → **feeling nothing** → **feeling great**

| -10 | -9 | -8 | -7 | -6 | -5 | -4 | -3 | -2 | -1 | 0 | +1 | +2 | +3 | +4 | +5 | +6 | +7 | +8 | +9 | +10 |

Mia monkey says 'cross your hands over your heart' in the heart healing position and take three deep breaths,

in and out,

in and out,
in and out.

Name your title 'Feeling grumpy'. Now copy Mia Monkey and do some magic tapping!

I am feeling grumpy.

Mia Monkey says tap the top of your head very gently 5 times.

So grumpy and cross.

Mia Monkey says tap the middle of your forehead very gently 5 times.

Sad and grumpy.

Mia Monkey says tap your inner eyebrow very gently 5 times.

I don't like feeling grumpy.

Mia Monkey says tap the side of
your eye very gently 5 times.

I release all this grumpiness into the clouds.

Mia Monkey says tap under your
eye very gently 5 times.

I wish I didn't feel grumpy.

Mia Monkey says tap under your
nose very gently 5 times.

Send all these grumpy feelings into the sky.

Mia Monkey says tap under your
mouth very gently 5 times.

Feeling less grumpy, aaaah, less grumpy.

Mia Monkey says tap your collarbone very gently 5 times.

Feeling happy and relaxed.

Mia Monkey says tap your thumbnail with another finger gently 5 times.

Feeling peaceful and calm.

Mia Monkey says tap your index fingernail with another finger gently 5 times.

Releasing all these grumpy feelings.

Mia Monkey says tap your middle fingernail with another finger gently 5 times.

I feel happy and smiley again.

Mia Monkey says tap your ring fingernail with another finger gently 5 times.

All these grumpy feelings drifting away.

Mia Monkey says tap your little fingernail with another finger gently 5 times.

Yeah, I'm feeling great!

Mia Monkey says tap your karate chop with another finger gently 5 times.

Now cross your hands over your heart into the heart healing position and take three deep breaths with Mia Monkey,

in and out,

in and out,

in and out,

then just relax.

Aaaah, that feels better. Mia Monkey says 'how are you feeling now'?

Hopefully you are feeling happy and relaxed, if you are now feeling happy, let that happy feeling into your little heart pocket in your imaginary safety vest.

Have a look at Charlie Chameleon's number scale, if you are still feeling a little bit grumpy and are still in the minus numbers then just repeat Mia Monkey's tapping lines a few more times until you feel happy again and you are in the plus numbers on Charlie Chameleon's scale.

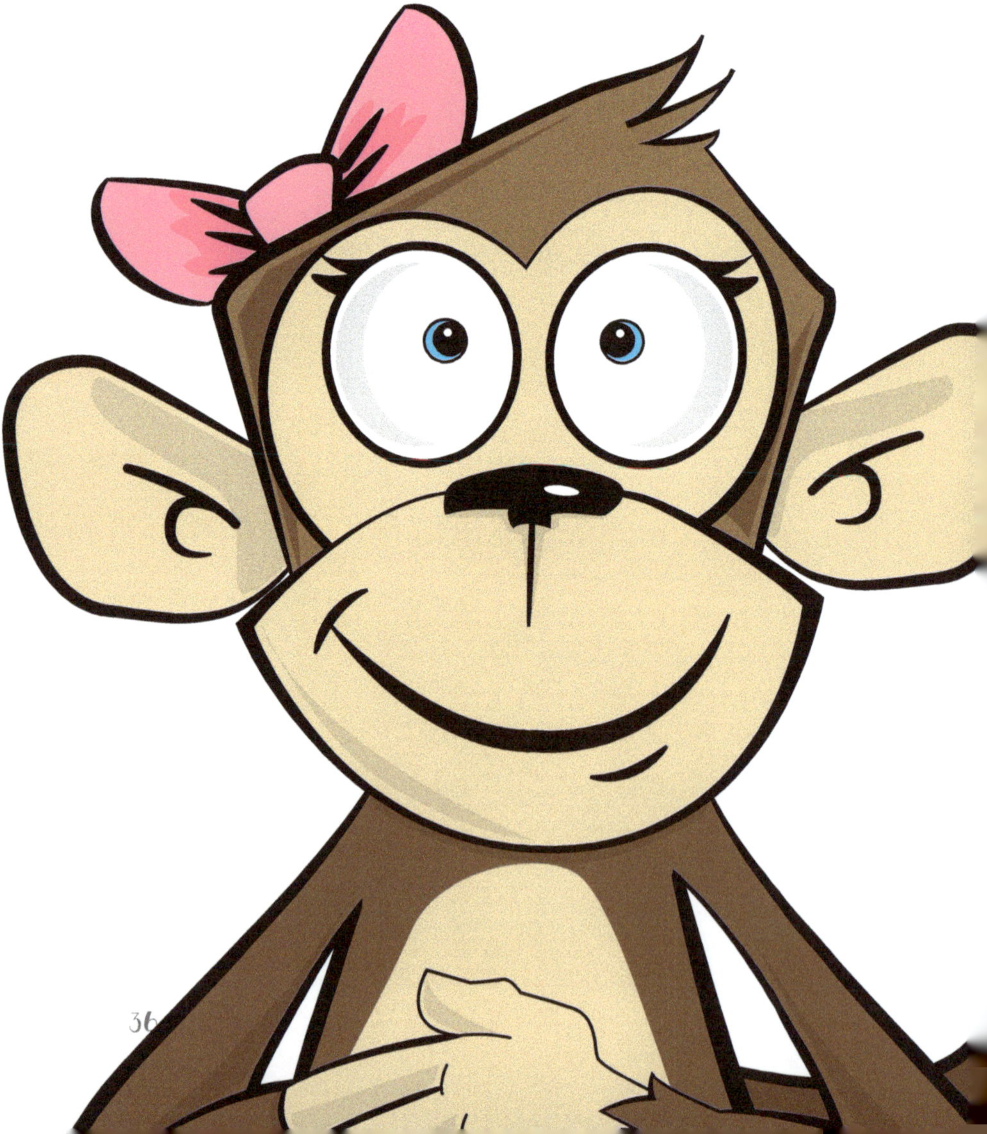

LITTLE ACCIDENTS

Mia Monkey says sometimes children can struggle to stay dry at night. Mia Monkey says don't worry, a little bit of Happy Tapping can help you to practice staying dry. Mia Monkey says 'put on your imaginary safety blanket', tuck it under your duvet to help you feel safe and snugly and tap along to make you feel better.

Mia Monkey says cross your hands over your heart in the heart healing position and take three deep breaths,

in and out,

in and out,

in and out.

Name your title 'I wish I could stay dry'. Now copy Mia Monkey and do some magic tapping!

I find it hard to stay dry at night.

Mia Monkey says tap the top of your head very gently 5 times.

I wish I could stay dry.

Mia Monkey says tap the middle of your forehead very gently 5 times.

It makes me feel sad.

Mia Monkey says tap your inner eyebrow very gently 5 times.

Its hard work staying dry.

Mia Monkey says tap the side of your eye very gently 5 times.

But maybe I could wake up if I need the loo?

Mia Monkey says tap under your eye very gently 5 times.

Then go back to sleep easily.

Mia Monkey says tap under your nose very gently 5 times.

I just need a little practice.

Mia Monkey says tap under your mouth very gently 5 times.

Practice makes perfect.

Mia Monkey says tap your collarbone very gently 5 times.

I could try to hold on a little longer in my sleep?

Mia Monkey says tap your thumbnail with another finger gently 5 times.

Mia Monkey says don't worry if you can't.

Mia Monkey says tap your index fingernail with another finger gently 5 times.

Staying dry takes lots of practice.

Mia Monkey says tap your middle fingernail with another finger gently 5 times.

Mia Monkey says it took her a while to learn.

Mia Monkey says tap your ring fingernail with another finger gently 5 times.

Just relax and enjoy your sleep.

Mia Monkey says tap your little fingernail with another finger gently 5 times.

Everything will be okay.

Mia Monkey says tap your karate chop with another finger gently 5 times.

Mia Monkey says 'cross your hands over your heart in the heart healing position and take three deep breaths',

in and out,

in and out,

in and out.

Aaaah, that feels better. Mia Monkey says 'how are you feeling now'?

Hopefully you are feeling happy and relaxed and safe in your snugly **imaginary safety blanket**.

Have a look at Charlie Chameleon's number scale. If you still feel a little bit worried about staying dry and are still in the minus numbers on the scale then just repeat Mia Monkey's tapping lines a few more times until you feel happy again and you are in the happy plus numbers on the scale.

Mia Monkey says 'let's try some 'Happy Tapping' to relax us so we feel safe falling asleep and not worry too much. It isn't hard, shall we try?

I am a very clever girl/boy.

Mia Monkey says tap the top of your head very gently 5 times.

I am great at going to bed.

Mia Monkey says tap the middle of your forehead very gently 5 times.

My bed is so comfy and warm.

Mia Monkey says tap your inner eyebrow very gently 5 times.

Mia Monkey says don't worry about anything.

Mia Monkey says tap the side of your eye very gently 5 times.

Just relax and go to sleep.

Mia Monkey says tap under your eye very gently 5 times.

Feeling safe in my snugly warm bed.

Mia Monkey says tap under your nose very gently 5 times.

Wrapped in my imaginary safety blanket.

Mia Monkey says tap under your mouth very gently 5 times.

I feel safe in my lovely bed.

Mia Monkey says tap your collarbone very gently 5 times.

I can wake up if I need the loo.

Mia Monkey says tap your thumbnail with another finger gently 5 times.

Feeling sleepy and tired.

Mia Monkey says tap your index fingernail with another finger gently 5 times.

Happy and relaxed.

Mia Monkey says tap your middle fingernail with another finger gently 5 times.

Peaceful and snugly.

Mia Monkey says tap your ring fingernail with another finger gently 5 times.

Drifting off to sleep.

Mia Monkey says tap your little fingernail with another finger gently 5 times.

Night, night everyone.

Mia Monkey says tap your karate chop with another finger gently 5 times.

Mia Monkey says 'cross your hands over your heart in the heart healing position', and take three deep breaths,

in and out,

in and out,

in and out.

Aaaah, that feels better. Check into Charlie Chameleon's scale and hopefully you are on the plus side of Charlie Chameleon's scale and feeling happy and relaxed and are drifting off to sleep.

feeling low → feeling nothing → feeling great

| -10 | -9 | -8 | -7 | -6 | -5 | -4 | -3 | -2 | -1 | 0 | +1 | +2 | +3 | +4 | +5 | +6 | +7 | +8 | +9 | +10 |

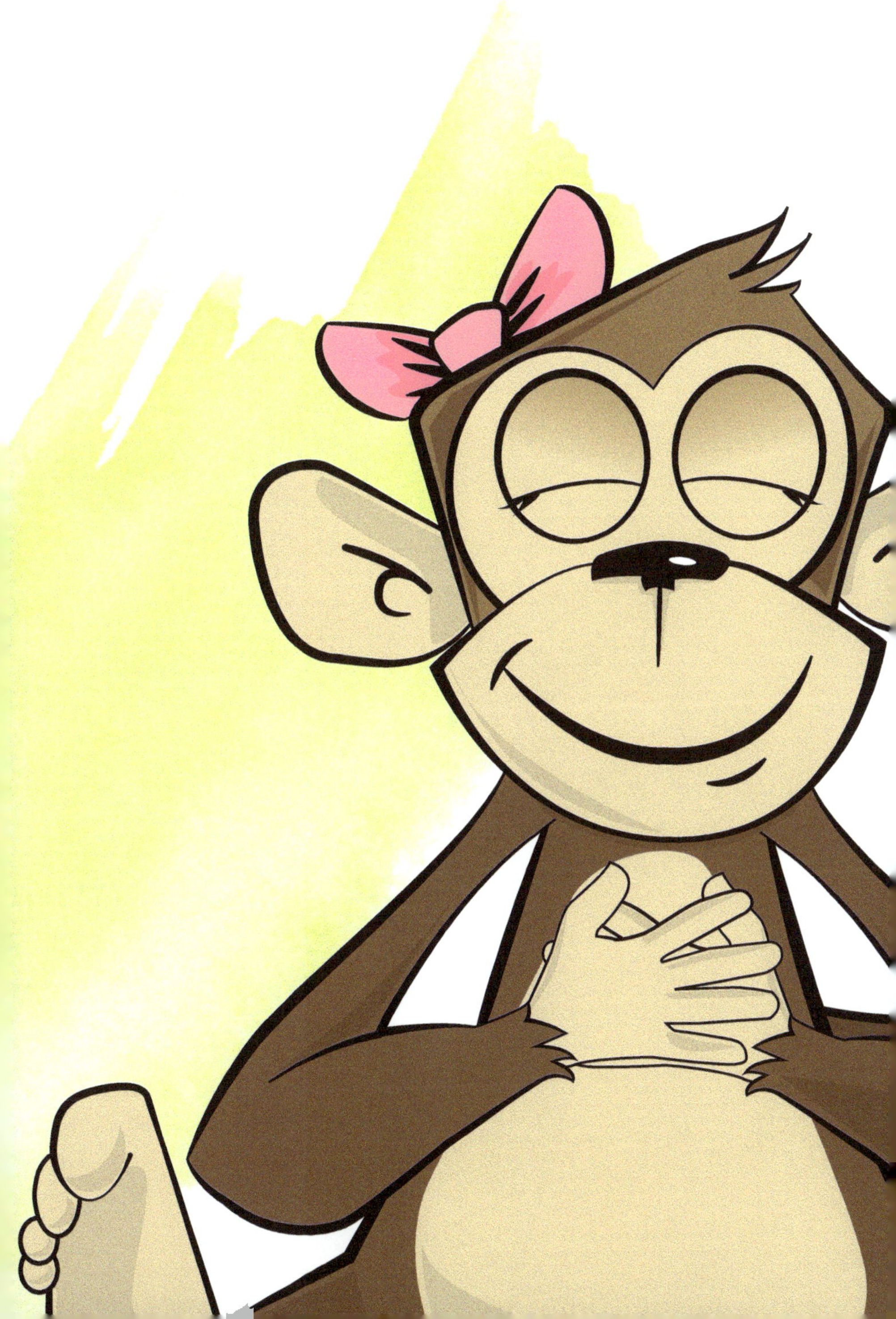

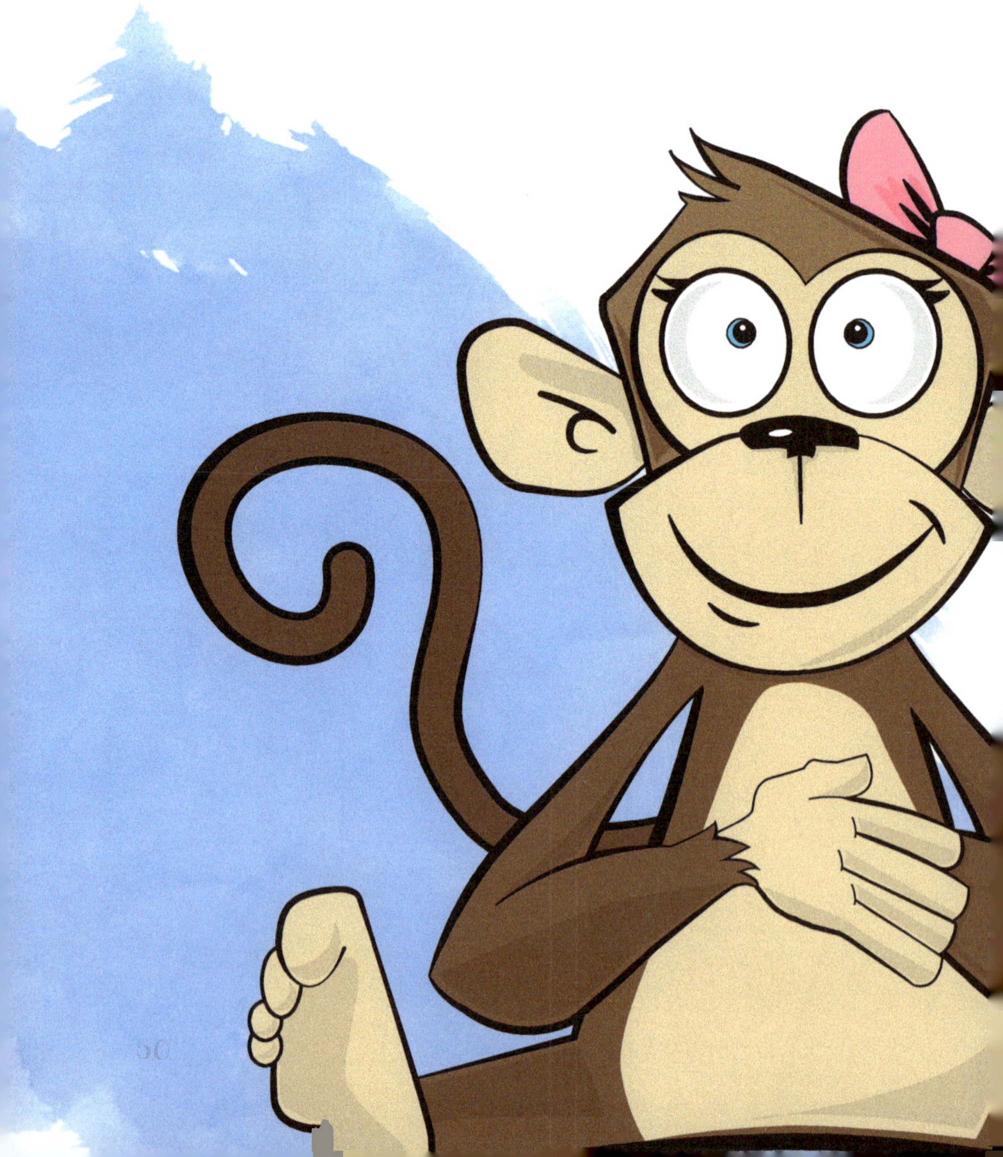

STARTING PRE SCHOOL/ SCHOOL

Mia Monkey says starting pre school/school can be a little bit scary for some children.

Mia Monkey says she can help us feel a bit better about going to school if we do a little bit of Happy Tapping. Shall we do some tapping with

Mia Monkey to help us feel a bit better? Mia Monkey says 'put on your imaginary safety vest to help you feel safe and secure and lets do some super tapping'.

Mia Monkey says 'cross your hands over your heart in the heart healing position and take three deep breaths',

in and out,

in and out,

in and out.

Name your title 'I want to stay at home'. Now copy Mia Monkey and do some magic tapping!

I don't want to go to school.

Mia Monkey says tap the top of
your head very gently 5 times.

I want to stay at home.

Mia Monkey says tap the middle of
your forehead very gently 5 times.

I want to stay at home and play with my toys.

Mia Monkey says tap your inner
eyebrow very gently 5 times.

Going to school sounds a little scary.

Mia Monkey says tap the outside
of your eye very gently 5 times.

Mia Monkey says it will all be okay.

Mia Monkey says tap under your eye very gently 5 times.

Mia Monkey says I am such a brave boy/girl.

Mia Monkey says tap under your nose very gently 5 times.

School can be lots of fun.

Mia Monkey says tap under your mouth very gently 5 times.

I will meet lots of new friends.

Mia Monkey says tap your collarbone very gently 5 times.

Maybe school will be fun after all?

Mia Monkey says tap your thumbnail with another finger gently 5 times.

I would like to give it a try.

Mia Monkey says tap your index fingernail with another finger gently 5 times.

I am such a brave boy/girl.

Mia Monkey says tap your middle fingernail with another finger gently 5 times.

I am sure it will be fun making new friends?

Mia Monkey says tap your ring fingernail with another finger gently 5 times.

Yeah, I am ready to try going to school.

Mia Monkey says tap your little fingernail with another finger gently 5 times.

I am quite looking forward to going to school.

Mia Monkey says tap your karate chop with another finger gently 5 times.

Now cross your hands into the heart healing position and take three deep breaths with Mia Monkey,

in and out,
in and out,
in and out,

then just relax.

Aaaah, that feels better. Mia Monkey says 'how are you feeling now, hopefully you are feeling happy and relaxed and ready to go to school'?

Have a look at Charlie Chameleon's scale, if you are still feeling a bit worried and are in the minus side of Charlie Chameleon's scale then do a few more rounds of 'Happy Tapping' with Mia Monkey until you are in the plus numbers on the scale.

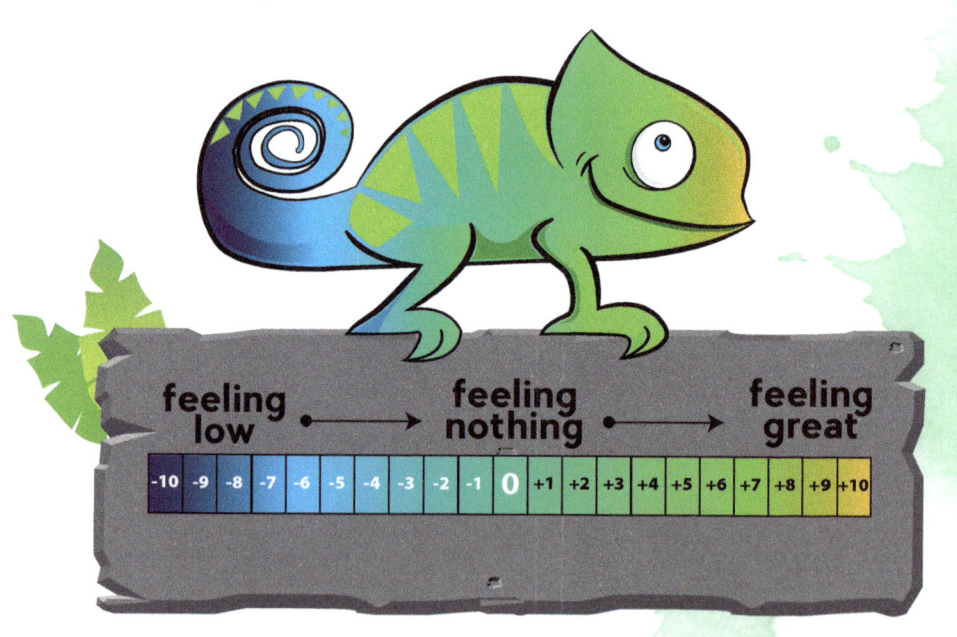

feeling low → feeling nothing → feeling great

-10 -9 -8 -7 -6 -5 -4 -3 -2 -1 0 +1 +2 +3 +4 +5 +6 +7 +8 +9 +10

Mia Monkey says 'you are such a brave boy/girl. Well done for doing all this super tapping'.

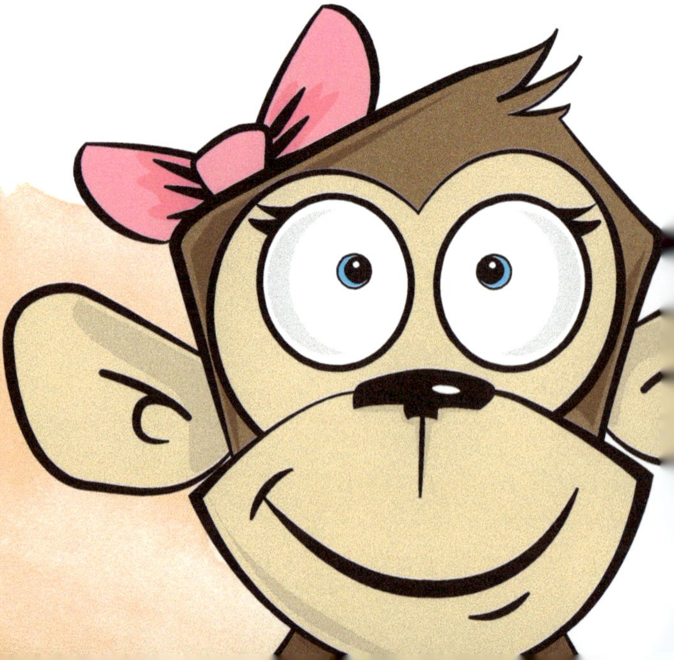

FRIENDSHIPS

Mia Monkey says making friends can be a little bit hard, especially if we are a bit shy, but Mia Monkey says once we make some new friends we can have so much fun with them. We can laugh and play, yippee it sounds like so much fun.

Mia Monkey also helps us with another script so if we were sadly to fall out with a friend it can help us feel better and hopefully make friends again or new friends.

Mia Monkey says 'shall we do some 'Happy Tapping' to help us feel more confident and a little less anxious about making new friends'? Put on your imaginary safety vest and lets get started.

Mia Monkey says 'cross your hands over your heart in the heart healing position and take three deep breaths',

in and out,

in and out,

in and out.

Name your title 'worried about making new friends'. Now copy Mia Monkey and do some 'Happy Tapping'!

I am a little worried about making new friends.

Mia Monkey says tap the top of your head very gently 5 times.

Mia Monkey says it will be okay.

Mia Monkey says tap the middle of your forehead very gently 5 times.

It's a big step making new friends.

Mia Monkey says tap your inner eyebrow very gently 5 times.

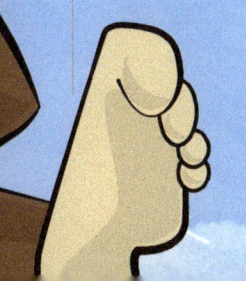

But it won't take long to learn.

Mia Monkey says tap the side of your eye very gently 5 times.

Even if it is a little scary to start with.

Mia Monkey says tap under your eye very gently 5 times.

Mia Monkey says she will help me feel less shy.

Mia Monkey says tap under your nose very gently 5 times.

Yeah, I can make new friends.

Mia Monkey says tap under your mouth very gently 5 times.

It will be lots of fun.

Mia Monkey says tap your
collarbone very gently 5 times.

Feeling ready to make new friends.

Mia Monkey says tap your
thumbnail with another finger
gently 5 times.

Yeah I can do this.

Mia Monkey says tap your index
fingernail with another finger
gently 5 times.

Making friends could be so much fun.

Mia Monkey says tap your middle
fingernail with another finger
gently 5 times.

Mia Monkey will help me to feel more confident.

Mia Monkey says tap your ring fingernail with another finger gently 5 times.

Looking forward to having new friends.

Mia Monkey says tap your little fingernail with another finger gently 5 times.

Having new friends will make me feel happy.

Mia Monkey says tap your karate chop with another finger gently 5 times.

Now cross your hands into the heart healing position and take three deep breaths with Mia Monkey,

in and out,
in and out,
in and out,

then just relax.

Aaaah, that feels better. Mia Monkey says 'how are you feeling now, hopefully you are feeling happy and relaxed and ready to make new friends'?

feeling low → feeling nothing → feeling great

-10 -9 -8 -7 -6 -5 -4 -3 -2 -1 0 +1 +2 +3 +4 +5 +6 +7 +8 +9 +10

Look on Charlie Chameleon's scale and see how you are feeling. If your number is less than a zero tap a few more rounds until you are happy about making friends and are in the happy plus numbers on Charlie Chameleon's scale.

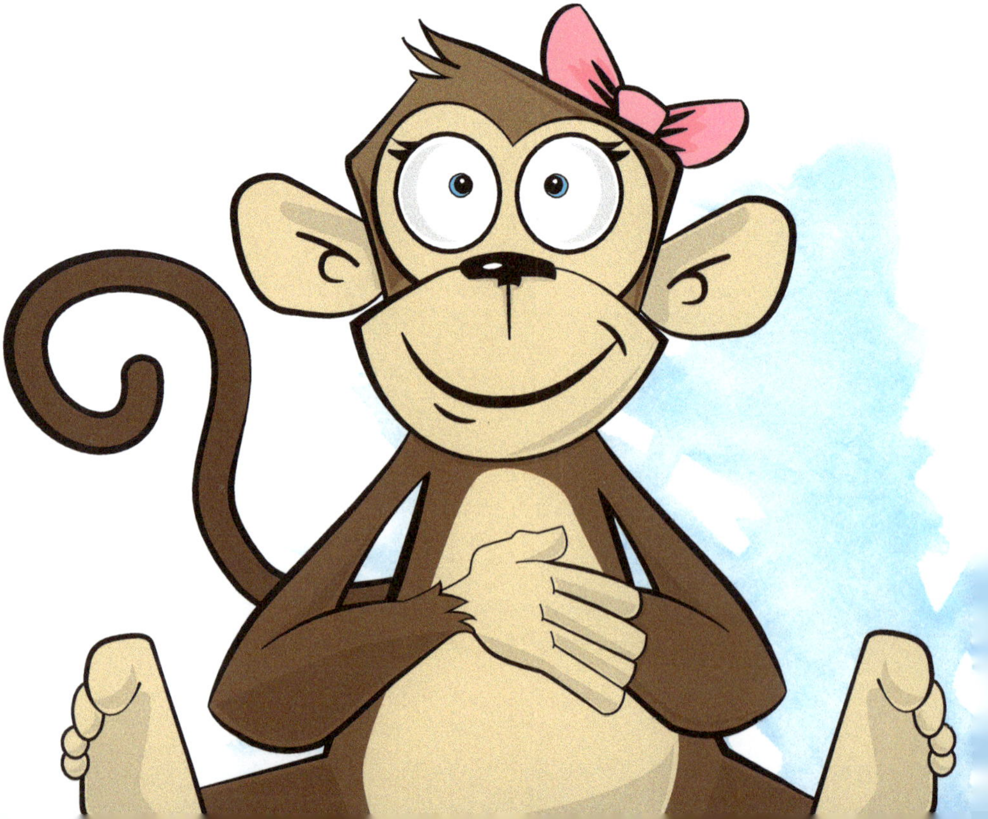

LITTLE FALLOUTS WITH FRIENDS

Mia Monkey says sometimes we can sadly fall out with our friends, she has written a tapping script to help you feel better if this happens to you. Shall we do some 'Happy Tapping' to help us feel much better and hopefully help us to make friends again?

This is a great time to put on your **imaginary safety vest,** just remember to shut the little door on any negative thoughts, words or feelings and let's get started.

Mia Monkey says 'cross your hands over your heart in the heart healing position and take three deep breaths',

in and out,

in and out,

in and out.

Name your title 'fallen out with my friend'. Now copy Mia Monkey and do some 'Happy Tapping'!

I am sad I have fallen out with my friend.

Mia Monkey says tap the top of your head very gently 5 times.

Mia Monkey says it will all be okay.

Mia Monkey says tap the middle of your forehead very gently 5 times.

I am feeling a bit lost without my friend.

Mia Monkey says tap your inner eyebrow very gently 5 times.

Mia Monkey says she will help you to feel better.

Mia Monkey says tap the side of your eye very gently 5 times.

Falling out with my friend has made me feel sad.

Mia Monkey says tap under your eye very gently 5 times.

Mia Monkey says she will help me make friends again.

Mia Monkey says tap under your nose very gently 5 times.

I could say I'm sorry to my friend if I accidently hurt his/her feelings?

Mia Monkey says tap under your mouth very gently 5 times.

Or tell them I am feeling sad if they have upset me?

Mia Monkey says tap your collarbone very gently 5 times.

Hopefully we can be friends again and have fun together once more?

Mia Monkey says tap your thumbnail with another finger gently 5 times.

Mia Monkey says I will feel better if I can sort this out.

> Mia Monkey says tap your index fingernail with another finger gently 5 times.

Maybe I can ask my Mum, Dad or a teacher to help me?

> Mia Monkey says tap your middle fingernail with another finger gently 5 times.

Feeling good about trying to make friends again.

> Mia Monkey says tap your ring fingernail with another finger gently 5 times.

Looking forward to making friends again or finding new friends.

Mia Monkey says tap your little fingernail with another finger gently 5 times.

Having my friend back or making new friends will make me feel happy.

Mia Monkey says tap your karate chop with another finger gently 5 times.

Now cross your hands into the heart healing position and take three deep breaths with Mia Monkey,

in and out,
in and out,
in and out,

then just relax.

Aaaah, that feels better. Mia Monkey says 'how are you feeling now, hopefully you are feeling happy and relaxed and ready to make friends again or find new friends'?

Look on Charlie Chameleon's scale and see how you are feeling. If your number is less than a zero tap a few more rounds until you are happy about making friends again and are in the happy plus numbers on Charlie Chameleon's scale.

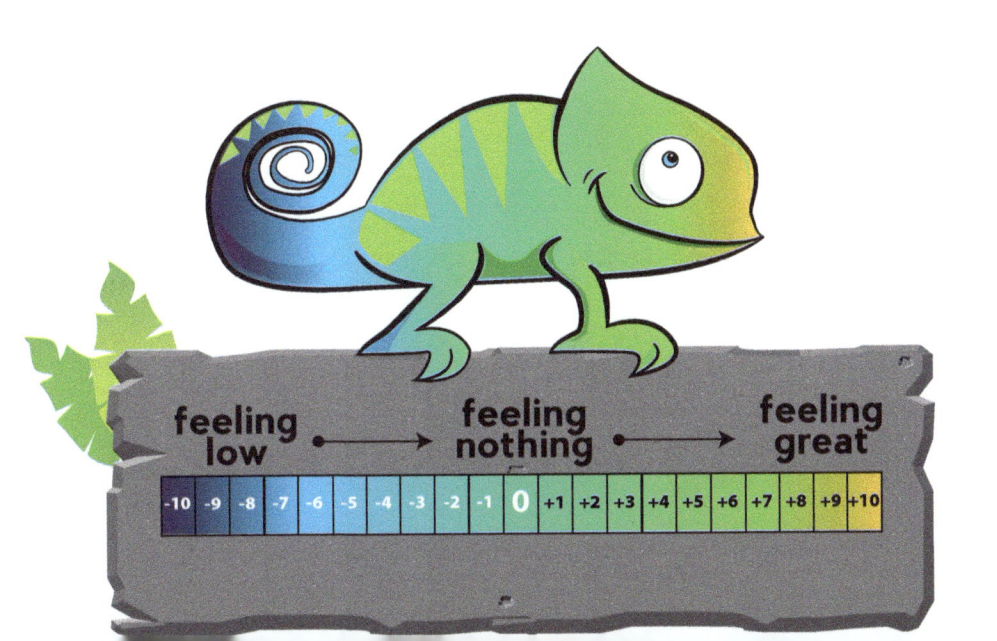

feeling low → feeling nothing → feeling great

| -10 | -9 | -8 | -7 | -6 | -5 | -4 | -3 | -2 | -1 | 0 | +1 | +2 | +3 | +4 | +5 | +6 | +7 | +8 | +9 | +10 |

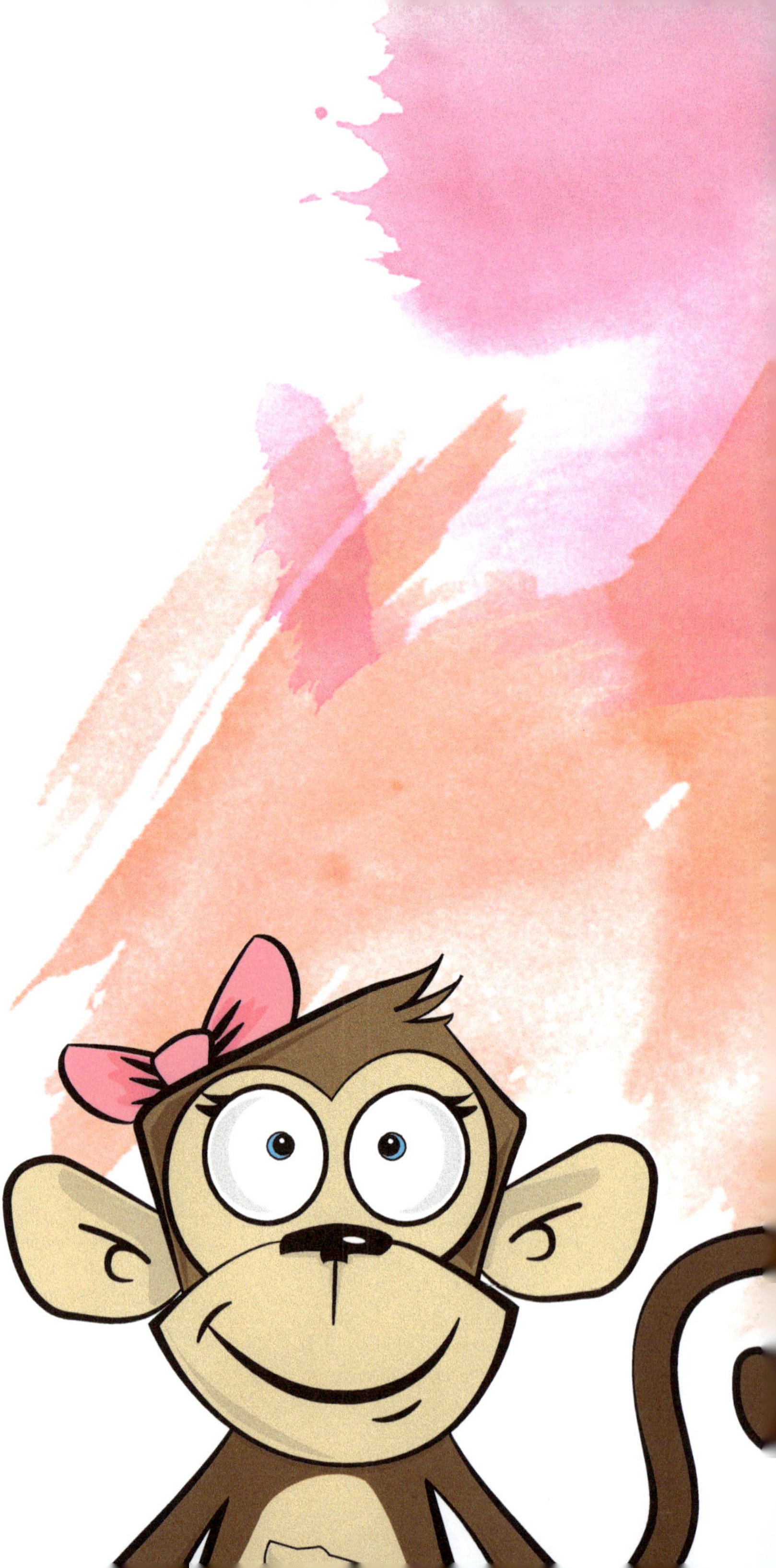

SEPARATION ANXIETY

Some children can find it a little bit scary to leave their house, all of their things and their family. This can sometimes happen when they go to school or to a new activity group, or to a friend's house that they don't know very well.

Mia Monkey says if you tap along with her it can help you feel a little bit better about getting out and about happily. Mia Monkey says zip up your **imaginary safety vest** and let's go.

Shall we do some 'Happy Tapping' with Mia Monkey?

Mia Monkey says 'cross your hands over your heart in the heart healing position and take three deep breaths',

in and out,
in and out,
in and out.

Name your title 'Worried about leaving my home'. Now copy Mia Monkey and do some Happy Tapping!

I am worried about leaving my Mum and Dad.

Mia Monkey says tap the top of your head very gently 5 times.

I would rather stay home and play with my toys.

Mia Monkey says tap the middle of your forehead very gently 5 times.

Leaving my house can be a little bit scary.

Mia Monkey says tap your inner eyebrow very gently 5 times.

Please let me stay home and play?

Mia Monkey says tap the outside of your eye very gently 5 times.

I am feeling a little anxious.

Mia Monkey says tap under your eye very gently 5 times.

Maybe I could try going to a friend's house?

Mia Monkey says tap under your nose very gently 5 times.

It might not be so hard?

Mia Monkey says tap under your mouth very gently 5 times.

Feeling safe and secure in my imaginary safety vest.

Mia Monkey says tap your collarbone very gently 5 times.

Maybe I could try, just for an hour or two?

Mia Monkey says tap your thumbnail with another finger gently 5 times.

I think I am ready to try.

Mia Monkey says tap your index fingernail with another finger gently 5 times.

I am ready to try new things.

Mia Monkey says tap your middle fingernail with another finger gently 5 times.

Mia Monkey will help me try.

Mia Monkey says tap your ring fingernail with another finger gently 5 times.

It could be so much fun.

Mia Monkey says tap your little fingernail with another finger gently 5 times.

I am a brave and clever boy/girl.

Mia Monkey says tap on your karate chop with another finger gently 5 times.

Now cross your hands into the heart healing
position and take three deep breaths with
Mia Monkey,

in and out,

in and out,

in and out,

then just relax.
Aaaah, that feels better.

Mia Monkey says 'how are you feeling now, hopefully you are feeling happy and relaxed and ready to be brave and try new things'?

Have a look at Charlie Chameleon's number scale, if you still feel a little bit worried about trying new things and are still in the minus numbers on Charlie Chameleon's scale then just repeat Mia Monkey's tapping lines a few more times until you feel happy again and you are in the happy plus side of the numbers on the scale.

feeling low → feeling nothing → feeling great

| -10 | -9 | -8 | -7 | -6 | -5 | -4 | -3 | -2 | -1 | 0 | +1 | +2 | +3 | +4 | +5 | +6 | +7 | +8 | +9 | +10 |

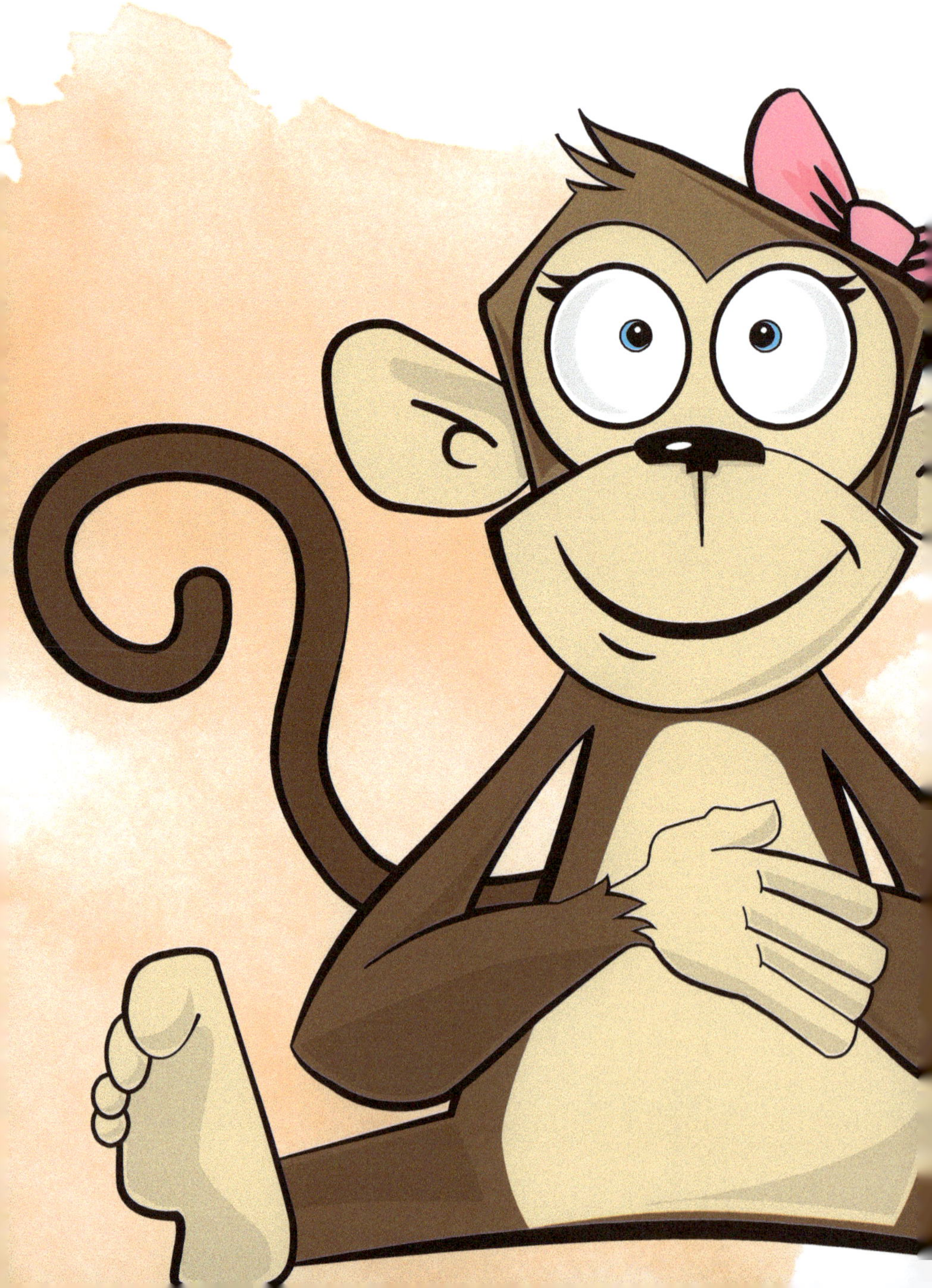

FEAR OF THE DARK

Mia Monkey says sometimes children can be a little bit scared of the dark.

Mia Monkey says she used to be scared of the dark too but with a little bit of 'Happy Tapping' Mia Monkey has learned not to be scared any more.

Shall we tap along with Mia Monkey to help us feel better when we are in the dark? Mia Monkey says 'put on your imaginary safety vest or your imaginary safety blanket if you are scared of the dark in bed, to help you feel safe and secure.'

Mia Monkey says 'cross your hands over your heart in the heart healing position and take three deep breaths,

in and out,

in and out,

in and out'.

Name your title 'I'm scared of the dark'. Now copy Mia Monkey and do some Magic Tapping!

I find the dark a bit scary.

Mia Monkey says tap the top of your head very gently 5 times.

I cannot see anything.

Mia Monkey says tap the middle of your forehead very gently 5 times.

It is a little bit scary.

Mia Monkey says tap your inner eyebrow very gently 5 times.

I wish I didn't feel scared in the dark.

Mia Monkey says tap the outside of your eye very gently 5 times.

I choose to feel safe in the dark.

Mia Monkey says tap under your
eye very gently 5 times.

Mia Monkey says I will be okay.

Mia Monkey says tap under your
nose very gently 5 times.

Maybe I won't feel so scared after all?

Mia Monkey says tap under your
mouth very gently 5 times.

But it is so dark.

Mia Monkey says tap your
collarbone very gently 5 times.

Wearing my imaginary safety vest or blanket to help me feel brave.

Mia Monkey says tap your thumbnail with another finger gently 5 times.

I choose to be very brave.

Mia Monkey says tap your index fingernail with another finger gently 5 times.

I choose to feel safe and secure in the dark.

Mia Monkey says tap your middle fingernail with another finger gently 5 times.

Mia Monkey will show us how.

Mia Monkey says tap your ring fingernail with another finger gently 5 times.

I am so brave for trying.

Mia Monkey says tap your little fingernail with another finger gently 5 times.

The dark can be pretty cool after all.

Mia Monkey says tap our karate chop very gently 5 times.

Now cross your hands into the heart healing position and take three deep breaths with Mia Monkey,

in and out,

in and out,

in and out,

then just relax.

Aaaah, that feels better. Mia Monkey says 'how are you feeling now, hopefully you are feeling brave enough to be happy in the dark'?

Have a look at Charlie Chameleon's number scale, if you still feel a little bit scared of the dark and are still in the minus numbers then just repeat Mia Monkey's tapping lines a few more times until you feel happy again and you are in the plus numbers on Charlie Chameleon's scale.

feeling low → feeling nothing → feeling great

-10 -9 -8 -7 -6 -5 -4 -3 -2 -1 0 +1 +2 +3 +4 +5 +6 +7 +8 +9 +10

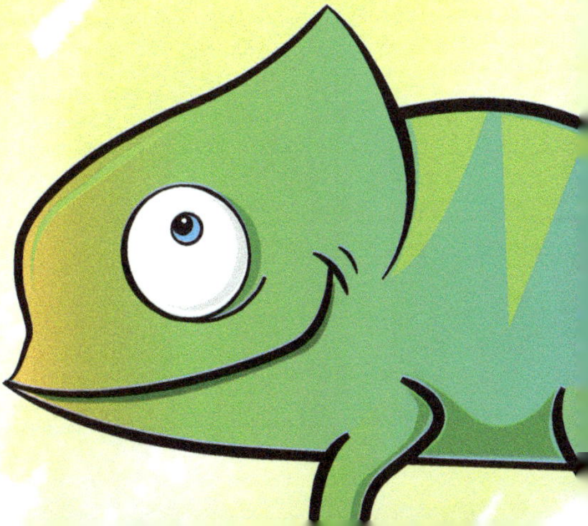

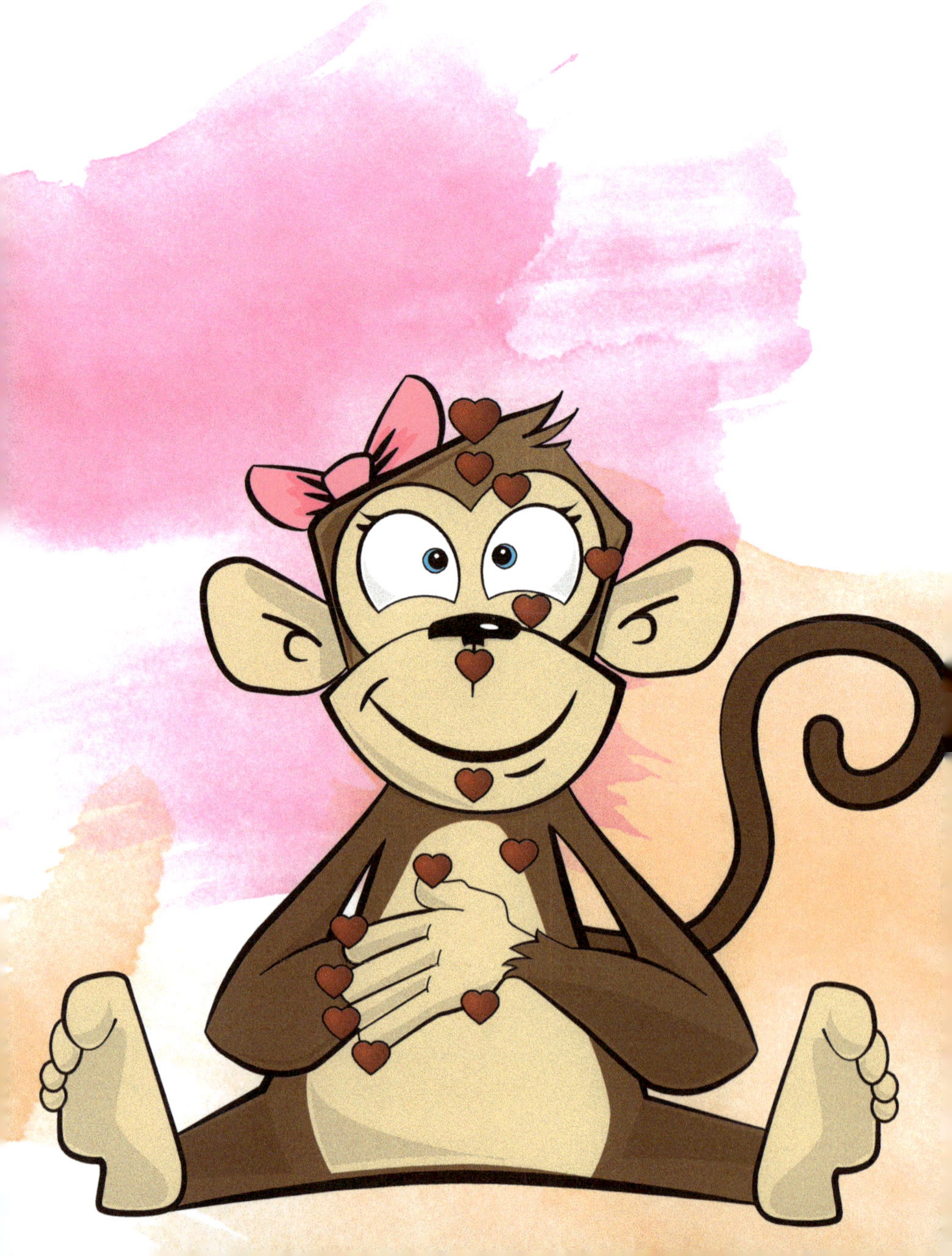

LOSING A PET

Losing a beloved pet can be a really sad experience in a child's life. Mia Monkey says she can help you to feel a little less sad about losing a pet if this should ever happen to you or if you have a friend who has lost a pet you could help them do some tapping. Mia Monkey says this is a great time to put on your imaginary safety vest or your imaginary safety blanket. Lock all the nice memories of your lovely pet into your little heart pocket and lets do some soothing tapping to help you feel better.

Mia Monkey says 'cross your hands over your heart in the heart healing position and take three deep breaths,

in and out,

in and out,

in and out'.

Now give yourself a big hug until you feel ready to do some gentle healing tapping. Name your title 'Losing my lovely pet'. Now copy Mia Monkey and do some soothing tapping!

I am feeling sad about losing my pet.

Mia Monkey says tap the top of your head very gently 5 times.

Mia Monkey says she will help me to feel a little less sad.

Mia Monkey says tap the middle of your forehead very gently 5 times.

But I feel so sad and will miss my lovely pet.

Mia Monkey says tap your inner eyebrow very gently 5 times.

It makes me want to cry.

Mia Monkey says tap the side of your eye very gently 5 times.

Mia Monkey says crying when you lose a pet is a good thing to do.

Mia Monkey says tap under your eye very gently 5 times.

It helps us to feel better and to process our feelings.

Mia Monkey says tap under your nose very gently 5 times.

So you feel lighter in your body.

Mia Monkey says tap under your mouth very gently 5 times.

Crying really helps us to let go of the pain we feel.

Mia Monkey says tap your collarbone very gently 5 times.

Letting go of all the pain and feelings of loss.

> Mia Monkey says tap your thumbnail with another finger gently 5 times.

Holding on to the good memories in my heart pocket.

> Mia Monkey says tap your index fingernail with another finger gently 5 times.

Letting go of all these sad feelings.

Mia Monkey says tap your middle fingernail with another finger gently 5 times.

Releasing all these sad feelings from my body and mind.

Mia Monkey says tap your ring fingernail with another finger gently 5 times.

Mia Monkey says give yourself a big hug for being so brave.

Mia Monkey says tap your little fingernail with another finger gently 5 times.

Letting go of sad feelings is a brave thing to do.

Mia Monkey says tap your karate chop with another finger gently 5 times.

Now cross your hands into the heart healing position and take three deep breaths with Mia Monkey,

in and out,
in and out,
in and out,

then just relax.

Give yourself another big hug to help you feel a little bit better. Mia Monkey says 'how are you feeling now, hopefully you are feeling a little bit better? she says be really kind to yourself and take it easy for a while, losing a pet is hard but you are doing really well for being so brave'. Mia Monkey says get all the hugs you can today from your friends and family.

Look on Charlie Chameleon's scale and see how you are feeling. If your number is less than a zero tap a few more rounds until you are feeling a little bit less sad try to get your number into the plus numbers on Charlie **Chameleon's scale so some of the sadness melts away into the clouds.**

feeling low → **feeling nothing** → **feeling great**

| -10 | -9 | -8 | -7 | -6 | -5 | -4 | -3 | -2 | -1 | 0 | +1 | +2 | +3 | +4 | +5 | +6 | +7 | +8 | +9 | +10 |

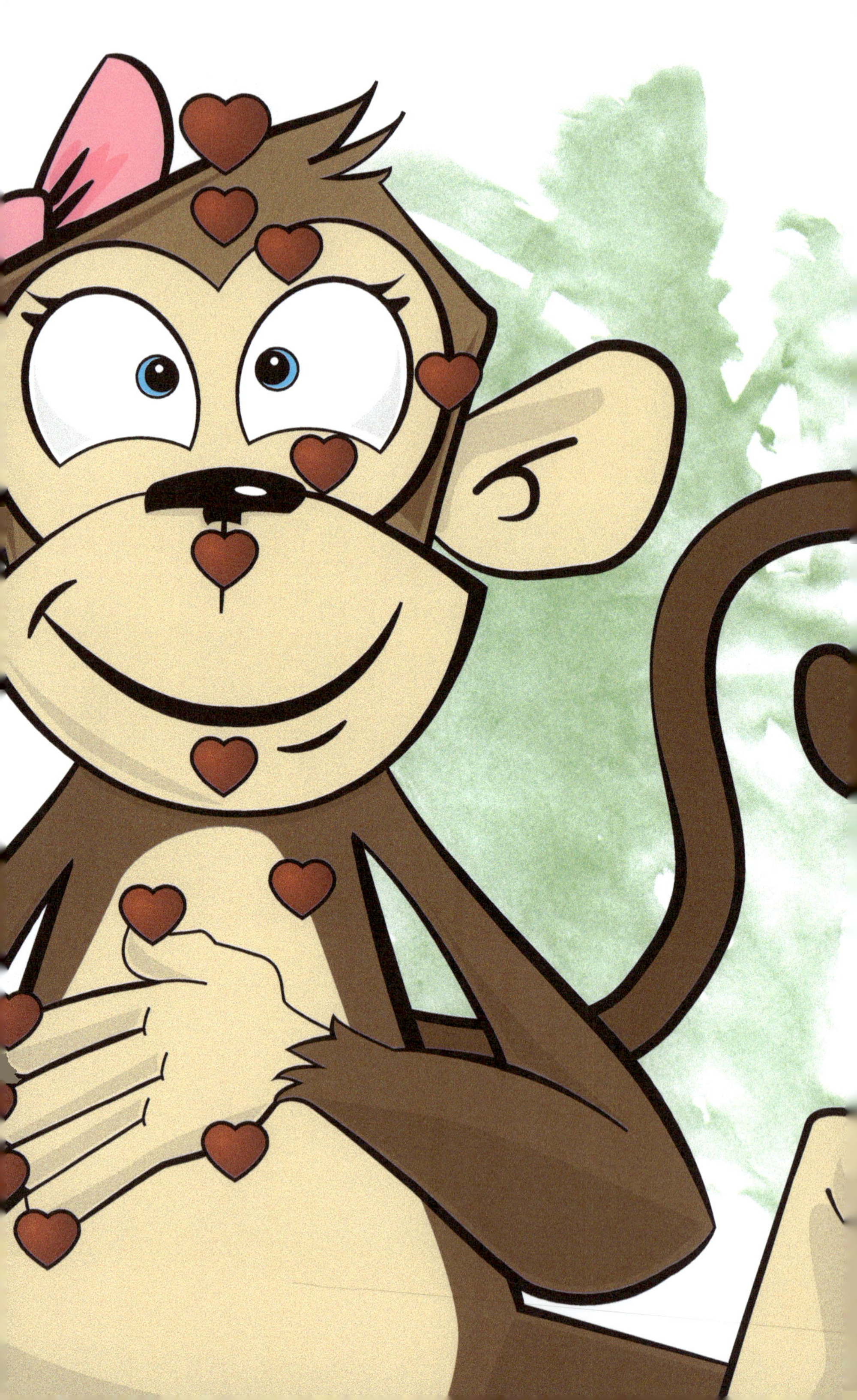

FEAR OF CREEPY CRAWLIES/SPIDERS

Mia Monkey says some children are a little bit afraid of creepy crawlies like spiders and bugs. Mia Monkey used to be a little bit scared too but she says some **'Happy Tapping'** can help us to feel a little bit braver when we see a spider or insect that is a little bit creepy.

Shall we tap with Mia Monkey to help us learn to not be so afraid of spiders and bugs? Let's put on our **imaginary safety vest** to help us feel safe around creepy crawlies.

Mum, Dad or brothers or sisters can tap along with us to this one if they are a little afraid of creepy crawlies too.

Mia Monkey says 'cross your hands over your heart in the heart healing position and take three deep breaths,

in and out,

in and out,

in and out'.

Name your title 'This fear of bugs and spiders'. Now copy Mia Monkey and do some magic tapping!

I am scared of spiders/bugs (name the insect you are scared of).

Mia Monkey says tap the top of your head very gently 5 times.

They have lots of scary legs.

Mia Monkey says tap the middle of your forehead very gently 5 times.

Some of them are hairy.

Mia Monkey says tap your inner eyebrow very gently 5 times.

Some have lots of eyes or wings.

Mia Monkey says tap the outside of your eye very gently 5 times.

Spiders and bugs are creepy and crawly.

Mia Monkey says tap under your eye very gently 5 times.

They scare me when they run really fast.

Mia Monkey says tap under your nose very gently 5 times.

They creep up on me and make me jump or fly around my head.

Mia Monkey says tap under your mouth very gently 5 times.

I am really scared of spiders/bugs (name the insect you are scared of).

Mia Monkey says tap your collarbone very gently 5 times.

They make me scream and shout for my Mum.

Mia Monkey says tap your thumbnail with another finger gently 5 times.

But what if I could learn to like spiders and bugs? (name your bug).

Mia Monkey says tap your index fingernail with another finger gently 5 times.

They don't have to be creepy after all.

Mia Monkey says tap your middle fingernail with another finger gently 5 times.

Maybe spiders /bugs aren't so bad?

Mia Monkey says tap your ring fingernail with another finger gently 5 times.

They could be pretty cool.

Mia Monkey says tap your little fingernail with another finger gently 5 times.

I choose to give them a chance to be cool.

Mia Monkey say tap your karate chop with another finger gently 5 times.

Now cross your hands into the heart healing position and take three deep breaths with Mia Monkey,

in and out,
in and out,
in and out,

then just relax.

Aaaah, that feels better. Mia Monkey says 'how are you feeling now, hopefully you are feeling brave enough to be around spiders and bugs'?

Look at Charlie Chameleon's number scale and choose a number relating to how you are feeling. If your number is less than zero tap a few more rounds until you are happy about spiders or bugs and are in the happy plus numbers on the scale.

feeling low → **feeling nothing** → **feeling great**

| -10 | -9 | -8 | -7 | -6 | -5 | -4 | -3 | -2 | -1 | 0 | +1 | +2 | +3 | +4 | +5 | +6 | +7 | +8 | +9 | +10 |

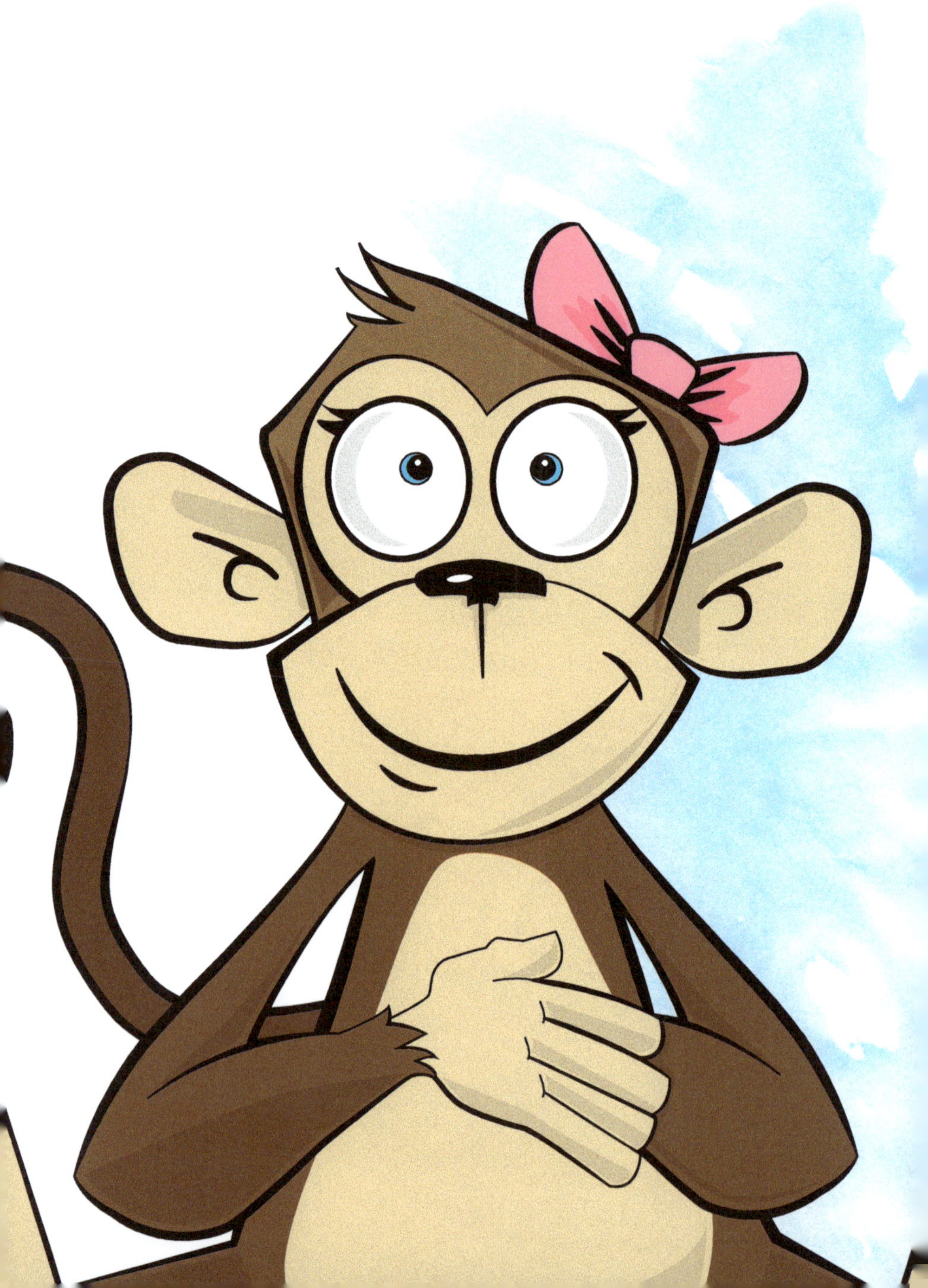

SILENT TAPPING

Mia Monkey says sometimes children can find it difficult to talk about what is bothering them. Mia Monkey says it is a great idea to do some silent tapping so children are able to feel better about what is bothering them and opening a window for talking about the problem later on when they feel more comfortable.

Mia Monkey says sometimes we can just tap on the feeling we have in our body, we may have butterflies in our tummy, a tight feeling on our neck or chest, or we may feel a little bit sick. Instead of talking about the problem Mia Monkey says it is just fine to tap on the feeling we have in our body instead.

Mia Monkey says 'let's put on our imaginary safety vest to help us to feel safe and secure and do a little bit of Silent Tapping.'

Mia Monkey says 'cross your hands over your heart in the heart healing position and take three deep breaths,

in and out,

in and out,

in and out,

name your title 'Silent Tapping',' now copy Mia Monkey and do some **Magic Silent Tapping**.

I don't want to talk about my problem.

Mia Monkey says tap the top of your head very gently 5 times.

But I can tap on the feeling in my body instead.

Mia Monkey says tap the middle of your forehead very gently 5 times.

This feeling in my tummy.

Mia Monkey says tap your inner eyebrow very gently 5 times.

This feeling in my chest.

Mia Monkey say tap the outside of your eye very gently 5 times.

This feeling in my head.

Mia Monkey says tap under your eye very gently 5 times.

I am worried about what is bothering me.

Mia Monkey says tap under your nose very gently 5 times.

Maybe I could tell someone how I feel?

Mia Monkey says tap under your mouth very gently 5 times.

But I don't feel like talking about it.

Mia Monkey says tap your collarbone very gently 5 times.

Mia Monkey says it's okay to tap silently.

Mia Monkey says tap your thumbnail with another finger gently 5 times.

Tapping silently can make me feel better.

Mia Monkey says tap your index fingernail with another finger gently 5 times.

So I can feel happy and relaxed.

Mia Monkey says tap your middle fingernail with another finger gently 5 times.

To help me feel calm and safe.

Mia Monkey says tap your ring fingernail with another finger gently 5 times.

Maybe I could tell someone how I am feeling?

Mia Monkey says tap your little fingernail with another finger gently 5 times.

Maybe it's okay to share my problems with someone I trust?

Mia Monkey says tap your karate chop with another finger gently 5 times.

Now cross your hands across your heart in the heart healing position and take three deep breaths,

in and out,

in and out,

in and out,

then just relax.

Aaah that feels better.

Look at Charlie Chameleon's scale and see how you are feeling. If your number is less than a zero tap a few more rounds until you are feeling happy and safe, and are on the plus side of the scale.

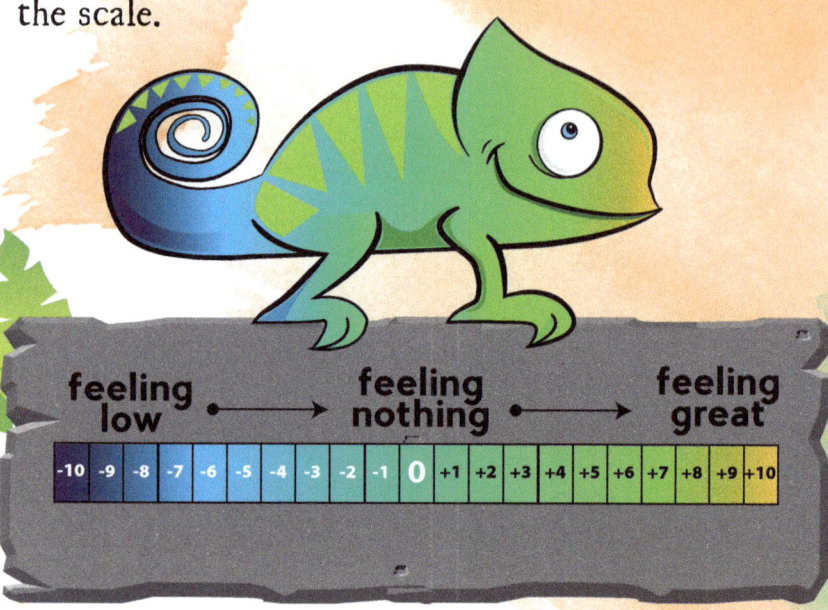

feeling low → feeling nothing → feeling great

-10 -9 -8 -7 -6 -5 -4 -3 -2 -1 0 +1 +2 +3 +4 +5 +6 +7 +8 +9 +10

Mia Monkey says 'do you feel ready to talk to someone about what has been bothering you?' Mia Monkey says it is good to share our problems with someone else as it helps us to let go of the things that bother us. Feeling safe and secure in your **imaginary safety vest** can help. Hopefully you are now in the happy plus numbers on Charlie Chameleon's scale and are feeling much better and are now able to talk to someone about your problem.

I hope you have enjoyed tapping along with Mia Monkey and Charlie Chameleon. Mia Monkey says just remember you can use you new 'Happy Tapping' skills any time you are sad, anxious, scared, lonely, worried, grumpy, tired, not tired, or if you just want a bit more energy. Mia Monkey says remember to put on your **imaginary safety vest, close your heart pocket to any negative words or feelings, and let in any nice words or feelings.** Happy tapping everyone.

Mia Monkey has written a little song for you to tap and sing along to.

Happy singing and tapping everyone.

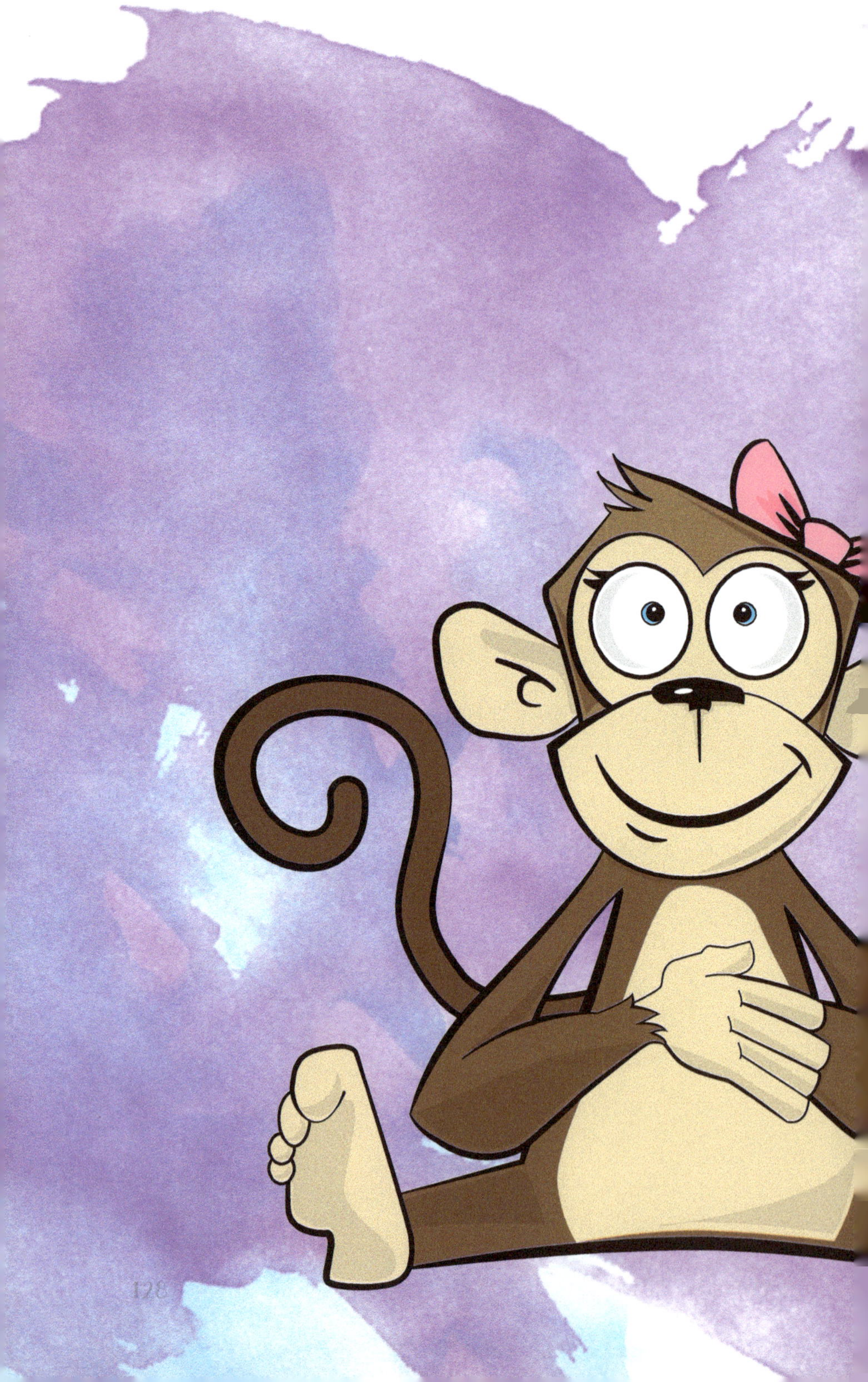

MIA MONKEYS TAPPING SONG

We tap on the top of our head,
before we go to bed,

We tap the centre of our forehead,
just like Mia Monkey said.

We tap our inner eyebrow, Mia
Monkey will show you how,

We tap the side of our eye, if we
ever need to sigh.

We tap under our eye, when
something makes us cry.

We tap under our nose, to feel as
happy as a rose.

We tap under our lips, if we're
anxious about taking trips.

We tap our collarbone if something
makes us moan.

We tap the side of our thumb, if
we're ever feeling glum,

We tap our index finger, so we're brave enough to be a singer.

We tap our middle finger nail, if someone tells a tale.

We tap our ring finger, when our grumpy moods linger.

We tap our little finger nail, when life feels a little stale.

We tap our karate chop, with a jump a skip and a hop.

Mia Monkey says lay your hands across your heart,

Take three deep breaths, so you feel really smart.

Lets all tap together, to make the world feel a little better.

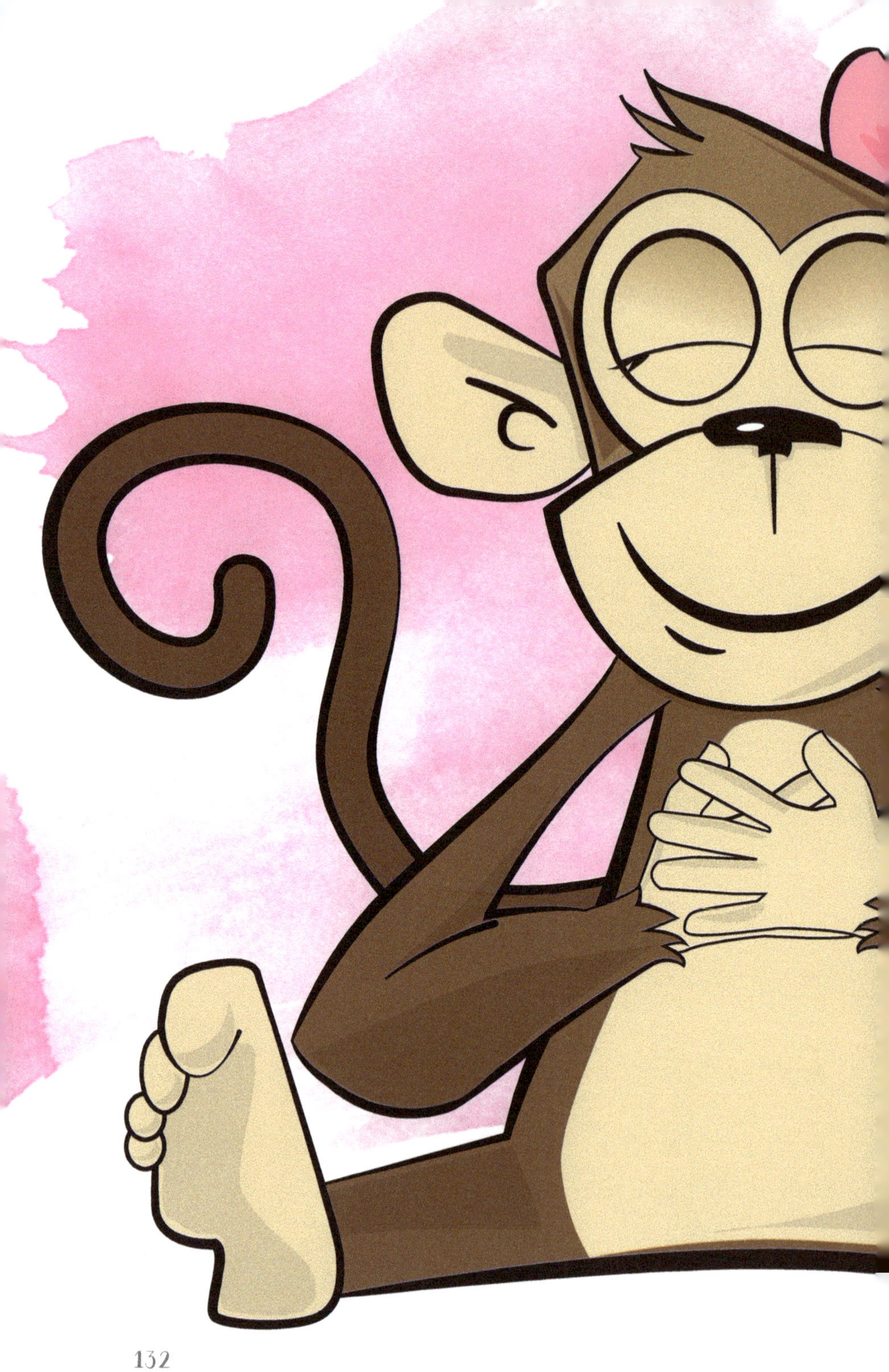

ADDITIONAL READING

Energy EFT For Teenagers

By Paula Kennedy is available on Amazon.